MW00639851

Being and Becoming Tezet:

Affirmations and Allowances

Tezet, Minkara
Being and Becoming Tezet: Affirmations and Allowances

ISBN 978-1-960886-00-2

Tezet Publishing LLC
Minneapolis, Minnesota, United States of America

Being and Becoming Tezet:

Affirmations and Allowances

by
Minkara Tezet

Dedication

Nala Potvin, you are the first reflection of myself I have shared with the world. Thank you for teaching me to live honestly.

Nia Ford, you are the reflection of the fullest potential I am sharing with the world. Thank you for teaching me to seek out purpose in my journey.

Bernice Christopher, you are the first reflection I discovered. In your being and becoming I have learned to become. Thank you for sharing life, love, and peace with me.

And,

On my Journey I take with me: prickles, goo, lusa, and Jesus too.

The Black - Kem

Akhepran — Created by the Creator

African — Created by the Motherland of Birth

African-American — Hyphenated to accept citizenship Human status in U.S.

African American — Created by Civil Rights Human Rights > Laws Of U.S.

Black American — Created by Liberation and Rebellion

Afro American — Created by Emancipation Left Over Conditions of Slavery

Negro — Created by the European

The Negro – an artificial, external identification giving rise to an internalized memory loss and cultural amnesia.

The social concept of the Negro was manufactured, was made possible, by the thinking of the European which is inadequate in its thinking of Being. This mode of thought is absent of Being-ness, Modoic Thought.

The Negro was seen as technology embodied in a human form, viewed as having been placed here to produce wealth for the dominant culture and civilization of another people.

We must know that an artificial intelligence (one absent of being) produced the Negro and a divine intelligence the African. The name African/Akhepran takes on the meaning of being, and becoming toward a union with the divine in Creation.

The Negro is one who is sanctioned as an earthly person, one who cannot think for her or himself. It's over, we are channeling thoughts of Creation to liberate our minds, escalate our thoughts, and to elevate our Being-ness (Azzahir, Azzahir, & Tezet 2019, 15).

Contents

Mission

Being and Becoming Tezet:
Affirmations and Allowances

The mission of Tezet is to support people in discovering the Self through the study of the self as a reflection of the divine presence in Creation.

Our desire is for people to see the benefit of using their skills and talents to support themselves, their families, and their communities.

Vision

Being and Becoming Tezet:
Affirmations and Allowances

The vision for Tezet is to develop a community for people to study ourselves in the course of our life's work. All people have knowledge intended to be shared from generation to generation. The knowledge that we as a people have is a resource that will give us the capacity to build and maintain community for ourselves. We realize the sharing of sacred practices, rituals, and ceremonies as a way of valuing the knowledge of our people.

Tezet sees the knowledge we share with one another as a community is our reinvestment in our people and peoplehood. We work to apprehend our natural capacity to establish a healthy cultural and psychological image of ourselves. We are working to produce knowledge as a community to support one another in the process of harvesting the knowledge from our experiences and the experiences of our people.

We realize the study of self and our people's knowledge are the keys to understanding our roles in creating a path toward familial healing and communal growth. Knowledge of self leads to the practice of self-development and the production of self-knowledge. Self-development and self-knowledge are the paths to transformation. We pray people discover the heart is the greatest instrument for transformation. We pray self-study leads people toward a collective vision of the Self as we work to create the conditions of spiritual harmony for the human community.

Affirmation of
Being Human

Being and Becoming Tezet:
Affirmations and Allowances

I am a human being.

I am in the process of being and becoming conscious of the Self.

I am a reflection of the divine presence in Creation.

I am listening for the Creator's call within my being.

The call I hear in my life is being reflected to me through Creation.

I am the living truth.

Khepra is being, becoming,
and transformation.

THE DEFINITION OF AFRICAN SPIRITUALITY

African spirituality is a conscious awareness of the Creator/ Creative Principle acting through Creation.

Introduction

Being and Becoming Tezet:
Affirmations and Allowances

Toward Khepra - Toward Transformation, Being, Becoming

My introduction into the mindset and consciousness of the concepts, ideas, and principles of Khepra and tezet comes from a Khepran Knowledge Philosophy, the philosophy of Khepra. My documented introduction to the philosophy was October 2, 2007, at the International Khepran Institute. "The International Khepran Institute was established in 1990 as a means of bringing together people of African descent to study and learn their spiritual and cultural heritage, and to consciously develop an intellectual culture to meet the ongoing changes that our people have experienced over the past 2,000 years," (Azzahir 2006, 5).

As I sat in the classroom at the International Khepran Institute, I sat in a new place and space surrounded by new thoughts, ideas, and ways of thinking. I was surrounded by symbols, books, paintings, and sculptures expressing a deep sense of Africanness. I experienced an Africanness filled with self-knowledge, self-respect, and self-reliance. In my mind this space felt like a sanctuary or a temple—the presence of something old and ancient was pulling me into the space. Class started with us doing a short check-in to introduce ourselves. Now as I look back through the thought of the moment, it is a fond memory. I was unaware of the relationships that would come from that evening—Seba Ahmad Azzahir, Elder Atum Azzahir, Shemsu Semerit SeAnkh-Ka, and Brother/Ancestor Mark Roberson were among some of the students and teachers who gathered for the teachings on this evening.

From the opening of the time together, I felt—both in my heart and spirit—I would never be the same. To know a thing, anything, is to study yourself and to know the world more intimately. So I sat, and I listened. The opening question that night was *Why study a Khepran Knowledge Philosophy?*

In my journal I copied down the four reasons:

1. Because it exists as a body of knowledge to be studied.

2. It gives knowledge to the basic universal understanding of African thought through understanding the actions and the motivations of the African.

3. The current state of the world requires that there be other ways of evaluating the state of crisis the world is in, through a different lens—one that moves beyond the logical view of Western thought to one which connects people to the earth and validation through "soul" connections.

4. To raise the overall level of awareness of the African. To enrich or validate that which is intuitively felt by African people on a cellular level—of knowing (Azzahir 2017, i-ii).

As I listened to the others in the class I was flooded with thoughts and questions—*What is a Khepra? What is Khepran? Who are Akhepran people?* In addition to these questions, at the top of mind for me was also the question of, *How is this applicable to my life and my life's work?* This question was at the top of mind because my life and life's work was what had led me to this place of seeking. As I listened, I could hear each of my questions being answered.

A part of relating or understanding each of these questions that were surfacing was tied to language and the practices related to cultural amnesia. I had never been introduced to the metu neteru, (hieroglyphs or sacred carvings) before this moment. I never really thought of the Egyptians as African or even about Egypt being connected to the continent of Africa. My mind was literally being blown by the thought of Khepra, and then Seba Ahmad carved the hieroglyphs for the word *tezet* on the green chalkboard. He drew it with a swiftness and a precision that seemed like something straight out of a storybook; this moment still feels legendary in my very being today.

As he drew the images from the metu neteru, he explained the meaning of the hieroglyphs as *self as a reflection of Creation.* I could not imagine how a cobra on a mound could translate into self as a reflection of Creation. While he was drawing the images, I found myself transported into another world. I found myself transported into a new way of thinking, and I thought, *How can these pictures mean self as a reflection of Creation? How does one come to see themselves as a reflection of Creation?*

This was, for the first time in my conscious awareness, an attempt to connect with the divine within myself—to my personhood, or to my peoples' peoplehood. *How are people (human beings) reflections of Creations?* For the first time, I was forced into thinking about the world in a different way—different than how I had been taught throughout my life to think about the world. I found a desire to see myself as a reflection of Creation. The rest of the class was full of thought-provoking teachings, but *tezet* was the teaching that stuck. I found myself captivated with the image of the serpent on the mound. I found myself thinking of the beauty and the wonder of a cobra sunning itself on a stone in the middle of a hot day, being at ease, and regenerating its energy.

Seeing Self as a Reflection of Creation

Khepra is a philosophy of transformation. Khepra teaches a process of being, becoming, and transformations. As I sat and listened in the class, I learned Black people, African people, Akhepran people, had taken symbols from creation to weave for themselves a story that allowed them to feel connected to the Creator and Creation. I was drawn into the teachings. The moment felt magical, and still today, as I type these words, I feel the truth of the moment—through the knowledge being shared with me, I was being filled with a sense of peace about my people and our heritage. In a moment, my world was flipped upside down—maybe, right side up.

Over the years, I have spent many hours reflecting on the questions of, *How am I a reflection of the cobra on the mound? What does this symbol and reflection have to do with peace and harmony? What does this symbol and teaching have to do with the conditions facing people of African heritage?* What I discovered for myself as I sat with these thoughts is I had a desire to experience the peace I imagined this being—sitting on a stone sunning—was experiencing. In my life, I wanted the same calmness and ease present in the glyph. I now realize I wanted a life where I could see the resonate consciousness of myself as *tezet.* It was in that first moment, I began to fantasize about being a reflection of creation; I felt I was spiritually and intellectually home within the Akhepran community.

In *Research and the Cultural Wellness Center,* Seba Ahmad writes, "It is the presence of the eternal in man's consciousness that Ancient Kemet called the *tezet* 🐍. This eternal is rooted in the hieroglyphs; it is a divine principle (or neter) on which the word functions. The word in ancient Kemet is made to function in the principle of the eternal" (Azzahir 2019, 34). *What does it mean to become conscious of yourself as an aspect of Creation that is eternal?* I found myself questioning the fabric of reality and wondering if I had the discipline to function in the symbology present; to function in what was being expressed through the mastery, peace, and discipline present for me in the image before me. *Tezet* has become a principle to study and anchors my life in a way of living, being, and becoming, as the eternal consciousness presenced through human beings.

At the time, I began to consider all these questions and thoughts. I did not have a sense of peace. I could not imagine a reality where I could have both access to peace *and* the capacity to make space for others to create peace for themselves. I began with a quieting exercise that would allow for me to write from my heart—I was searching for a voice of calm in myself. The aim was to make space for the peace of life to be present.

A Path to Peace

In addition to learning about the metu neteru through the International Khepran Institute, another part of our learning journey was seeing writing as part of our path to peace. The path to peace (hotep), as I was learning from this class, is the process of being and becoming aware of the transformation taking place around me. I was unaware of my Khepra before this point. I was not conscious of the path of Khepra as a way of being. I was learning to be conscious of myself as a human being and all it meant to be human.

I continue to discover inner peace through the process of studying the patterns of my daily life and living. I've always wanted to see myself as a good man, as a good person, a good human being. I have also always wanted to see myself as a wise person. It was in letting go of this thinking, I have learned each person has the ability to advance our collective efforts to heal and build community on the planet. Each person must study themselves to realize the truth of our own states of goodness or wisdom.

The study of Khepra took me to the place where I had to learn to live with myself. Azzahir (2017, 16) states, "Khepra deals with the personalized, spiritual journey of the individual; that journey is explicated in the heart-soul and the experiences that enrich its existence." I am still learning to realize this relationship with myself and the cosmos. This philosophy has given me access to thoughts about being I had never imagined. I was imagining and sitting with thoughts like, *how does one live in alignment with the universe* and *how does one learn to sit with thoughts of eternity or immortality.*

The Beginning of Listening to My Heart

Early in the learning process with Seba Ahmad taught, *each person has to produce a body of literature on behalf of our people.* I took this to mean I had to write something—anything—every day, and that the knowledge I produced must be for the advancement of our collective experience as people of African heritage. The thought of writing everyday and producing a body of literature was not easy for me to digest. I had come to despise writing because of my experiences in academia and professionally; writing was filled with pain and suffering and often felt useless.

The charge behind Seba's instructions gave me the push and drive to see writing each day as a part of my personal responsibility to produce a body of literature on behalf of our people. His statement was about seeing the body of literature we have the potential to produce as knowledge for future generations; knowledge about us living up to our collective responsibility to tell the stories of how we how we made it through life's challenges. The thought of writing every day as tasked toward producing a body of literature on behalf of my people felt difficult, but I am working towards it.

As I look back on the writing assignment and my pursuit of peace, I was working to see myself in relationship with the circles and the cycles of life and living, as my Ancestors did. At the time I was not aware of this, but as I am sitting with myself this very evening writing down these words, I am now aware of myself being in relationship with something beyond imagination. Life is beautiful here, and as I learn to see the truth in being a reflection of the divine in Creation, I have peace. I am striving to be at peace with my life and the cycles of being and becoming.

I am discovering how to sit in the realization of having the capacity to channel the Creator's presence through being. I feel as though some might read these words and think I am claiming to be something extraordinary, but this is the furthest thing from the truth. I do not feel special for the learnings and the teachings I have discovered—I am grateful to know we are all extraordinarily human. It is this sense of gratitude that helps me to be present in myself each day as I find myself wrestling with the mundane.

As I continued to see my life as a process that allows me to see myself as a human being, I was realizing the beauty in being able to tell a story and to share my thoughts with the people I cared for most. My process of self-discovery was anchored in my practice of writing six sentences each day. The sentences began the way I spent time writing. The practice of *creating a space for presence*—the writing of six sentences each day was the way I began to learn how to give attention to my breath. I began to see the experience of taking time to be with the presence of the divine and what the presence was teaching me.

I realize, now more than ever, the world is not run by the material or the objective reality we live in, but it is deeply impacted by and connected to the invisible realities of culture and spirituality. Seba explains,

> "The knowledge philosophy of contemporary Africa, the Africa that remains untouched by Western education, maintains this experiential rootedness through which the philosopher achieves a metaphysical and cosmological understanding of the universe as well as the principles behind its manifestation. But here is the *process*—the experiences that an individual has had, and that he reflects in his being and the way he lives his life—that endows him with the status of philosopher (shaman, metaphysician, mystic, Sufi, soothsayer, etc." (Azzahir 2017, 63).

This was not my aim—I was only entering into my inner self to hear the Self. I realize today I was in search of a way of thinking and being that allowed me to find relief from the pain and suffering I was experiencing. I was in search of a life that felt connected to something inside myself and out in the world.

In retrospect, I realize I was beginning the practice of *creating a space for presence* to have peace on the small pieces of earth I occupied as I am moving through my life. Today, I realize the conditions of my life and experience of life as I started this study could be best described as miserable. My life, in so many ways, had become unbearable. A Khepran Knowledge Philosophy was a way out of the stress and anxiety. A Khepran Knowledge Philosophy was a way of thinking and being that gave me a sense of freedom to be myself and become what the Creator had called me to be. I am learning to understand the teachings that come from the heart, give us access to the divine. I am learning to establish a sense of peace and ease in my life. As I began to be with the peace and ease of my life I began to apprehend my heart's utterances as I wrote down my thoughts and feelings. I was learning the power of prayer.

The Power of Prayer

I feel myself wanting to laugh as I write the words, *power of prayer.* I realize now many of my thoughts and feelings were unacknowledged prayer. My mother taught me our thoughts and our feelings are full of power. I never thought I would be one who would be expressing such thoughts—partly because my training in the professional world and in the academy had made me cynical about religion and religious practices. Learning the power of prayer from my mother reoriented me from religious dogma to the practice of spirituality. I was cynical and bitter, which is why I desired peace so much. The bitterness forced more isolation, because the more I could not trust the hearts of other people, the less I could trust myself.

As I watched my mother in the last years of her life, I allowed myself to give into the desire to write. My mother, Bernice Christopher, was a woman of prayer—it was her gift, and it was the gift she shared freely with others. I watched as she used prayer as a way of being present with the divine. I watched as she worked with each of her life struggles to have peace despite how unbearable life could feel. She used prayer no matter how much pressure seemed present. The time with her words, the sound of her voice talking to the Creator, gave her what appeared to be peace and ease in her life.

My mother's prayer life consisted of peace and ease. My mother was teaching me the practice of peace and ease through her life and living. While she lived her everyday life, she was teaching me to see how the Creator was able to express presence through our hearts. She also taught me to see how each of us could have a personal relationship with the divine presence in Creation. Writing daily was the path for me to achieve presence with the Creator. *Creating a space presence* began to allow me to hear how the divine in Creation expresses peace to itself.

I would wake up each morning before my daughters and write. I would allow myself the space to be in the presence of whatever feelings, senses, or thoughts wanted to come through. I was learning then, and still learning now, sitting still to allow yourself to hear the thoughts and feelings, gives us the ability to hear solutions for our lives. When we open our hearts to the Creator and offer our voices to Creation, the universe is listening. I watched my mother live a prayerful life, and as she prayed, I watched her use the instruction that came through as she emptied herself of the gratitude she had for living.

"In all things be grateful," she would say. "You can hear God speak when you let go of your fear. When you are able to trust the voice of God within you, you can't lose. You have to trust it with everything you have." Her words helped me to see being grateful is about realizing the gift is having time to live a better life. Her words helped me realize the gift is in making time to be with the people you love and care for and to be with those who love and care for you too.

Listening to the Heart

One of the gifts of learning to listen to your own thoughts and feelings is you learn to listen to how and what other people are thinking and feeling. Listening does not happen in some mystical way—and yet, in some aspects, there is a mysticism in learning to listen. As I learned to listen to myself, I could hear and see I was not alone in this depressed place I found myself wrestling with in life. I was not the only person living with these feelings. I was understanding each of us has a way of learning, unlearning, and relearning that adds to our ability to live in harmony with ourselves and other people—this is a teaching I hold close to my heart. In learning to love and care for the people closest to me I began to listen to the heart. I was learning to listen to my own heart.

In learning to listen to my heart, and learning to tolerate the sound of my voice, I was learning to accept how the Creator and Creation shows presence through each of us. We are all learning to listen to our hearts. And, I was learning to trust my heart. We are all learning to be with the sense of hope or despair our experiences are producing. I was learning how the Creator/Creative Principle was acting through me. I was learning to practice the primary tenet of African spirituality, having a conscious awareness of the Creator/Creative Principle acting through Creation.

It was in realizing I was operating out of a sense of the mundane, rote, and routine aspects of life that made my life feel miserable. There was no breaking out of the day-to-day and there was no escaping the life I had created for myself. My days felt long and endless. I felt absorbed by life. My life did not feel stellar or spectacular—it was regular—every day I felt like this, and I hated it. At the same time, I worked to make it through. At times, I worked harder because working harder felt like it was easing the process somehow—it felt like I might somehow reach the goal faster, but there did not seem to be any end. I only reached more work and more spinning on the hamster wheel of life.

As I fast forward into the present, I am grateful I survived those times. There is a lot of pain in holding those memories. There is a lot of suffering in those thoughts, and in some ways, the suffering is what I was striving to get out of. I was in search of a way to exorcise the misery, pain, and suffering. I was in search of a way to make sense of the life I was experiencing. I thought to myself, *this cannot be as good as it gets*. I was convinced there was a way to transcend the challenging feelings I had attached to the daily practice of my life at the time.

I have had to work hard to relate to myself in a way that allowed me to make peace with living in the moment. In becoming conscious of how I was living and how I wanted to live, I realize now my experiences with life so far were about learning how to tell the story I am in. Learning to sit with my composition notebook and pen, opened me up to a place where I could, for a moment, escape the mundane. Writing and meditation are the places that allow me to simply be present with myself without pressing myself for more. I learned to let the words come through and express the truth of the space and experience I found myself in. I am learning to allow myself to teach myself from moment to moment. I have learned to allow myself to intentionally take time to become mindful of myself to have the greatest harmony with the people who are closest to me.

In sitting with the sentences I wrote in the early part of my journey, I learned to make peace with the routine and mundane of life. What I mean is, I was working to see there were teachings in all the experiences I was having. I was learning to value each of the teachings. I was learning to see there was peace in *all* of being. For me the study of Khepra, has taught me to realize we are all on a path and the path we are on is a path of transformation that leads to peace with yourself - to peace with your ways of being and becoming. The other day, I came across these four sentences that talk about the path of Khepra in *The Three Books of Khepra* (Azzahir 2017, 217-18):

The path of Khepra is nothing but your journey to your original state, journeying across the great stream of time and death into a region of harmony.

The path of Khepra is a living one, infinitely adaptable to the individual natures but also infinitely discerning and discriminating in appraising those who seek to profess to seek it.

The path of Khepra teaches a mastery of the celestial powers and how to realize an immortal body no longer subject to molecular dissolution.

The path of Khepra demands of one to reflect consistently in a corresponding self-attunement with one's own behavior, because our actual creed is inseparably made to manifest in how we behave, regardless of what anyone may verbally process.

These sentences gave me a great sense of peace, and at the same time they are the greatest challenge to me. They are a reminder to see myself and to see my people—acknowledging and seeing the experiences we have had and to see how we have survived. I am working to live a life of attunement that allows me to see the conditions we share are not ours alone.

Trusting the Process - Trusting the Heart

We are all, learning to be in relationship with life beyond routine daily living. The practice of *creating a space for presence* allows me to have a conscious relationship with the Creator. This relationship feels like a gift. I remember sitting on the patio of my apartment the summer of 2013. I remember sitting each morning diligently with my pen and journal. Each time I wrote the six sentences I could feel the ease the moment produced. I can still feel the release that pulled me back to the pen. The process was intoxicating - just the release of the words. As I would read the words back to myself, I could feel the peace of letting go of life for a while—and that's how I would hear the old folks talk about prayer and meditation—they could feel themselves let go and the words would just flow with the power of releasing and being at peace with God.

Peace as a power taught me to see life is not just about today. It also taught me life is not just about the pains and the woes of yesterday—life is about learning to live in harmony; living in harmony with ourselves, the people closest to us, and with the planet. Life is a collection of experiences we are all having. I was realizing I had the ability to transcend the presence of my personal bitterness through studying myself with the power of peace in mind.

Writing is my first love—and painting has become a second. Through writing I am able to see how we can turn the excrement of life, the shit of life, into a beautiful life worth living; each sentence written is a line towards peace beyond the shit of it all. *Becoming Tezet* was one of the first self-study journals I produced the summer of 2013. It did not feel like a body of work I could define as a 'body of literature', but it was a start. It was a start towards being intentional in allowing myself to be present with my thoughts, words, and deeds. The words were short and brief. The impact of the thirty minutes in meditation, which led to the writing of the journal, was divine.

Now, I can see how I was working to know myself and to further develop myself as a human being. I began the practice of anchoring myself in my ability to be centered. I anchored myself by writing six sentences each morning as a part of my daily ritual of learning to listen to myself, and to listen to what I had learned about attaining peace and being free.

To give life is to offer love. Share your life with others so the world can have peace. To have light in yourself is to give love. Offer your light as a whole being. Remember your inner child in a world where people are distracted by their own reflections. Seek the source of Creation and know being is real.

These are the thoughts and feelings that came from me learning to play an active role in developing the knowledge my life has to offer. In being instructed to produce a body of literature, I heard Seba telling us all it was our responsibility to share the knowledge of our life experiences.

Creating a Self-Study

It has been in the process of self-study I have come to see how I have produced the life I live. No matter what I say, it is what I do that is going to get me into the life I hope to have with myself. I am learning to take ownership of my ability to have peace and to be at peace with others, especially with those closest to me. The words expressed in this self-study journal are from my first journal of affirmations, when I was in search of a true voice—I was in search of *my* true voice.

I have learned through my study that, "In spiritual matters he who can be discouraged is not worthy of encouragement. It is by means of discouragement that mediocre minds are eliminated." This quote is from the *Ruit Net Sebaut – the Tablet of Instructions* (Azzahir, Azzahir, & Nefer-Ra, 2003). It has become a sacred document for my own self-study, helping me understand the instructions that come from being conscious and aware that you are in a divine relationship with the Creator of all Creation. I have learned if I can discourage myself, I can be easily discouraged.

At the time I began this journal, I was beginning my journey inward. I did not know I was learning to encourage myself, but I was. I realize now I was giving myself permission to consider the original nature of Black people before colonization. I was giving myself permission to consider the state of being Black in America from a different lens. This was the path I had embarked on—I wanted to know myself as a spiritual being. Up until this point in my life, my only spiritual reference was practiced within the context of Christianity. I searched the Bible and the theologians of the Bible to hear who I was - who we were as a people. I was in search of myself then, just as much as I continue the process of searching and examining my ways of being on a daily basis as a practice now.

I learned from studying the historical personality called Jesus—or in the Ren-n-Kem (speech of the Black)—Iusa. In discovering a way to culturally translate the personality or principle of Iusa as the coming sun, I was able to see the truth in the rising of the sun. I was able to see this truth through the cycles and seasons of life, while also considering the life cycle of a child being born. I began to see how the passing of time was impacted by my intention to become conscious of my time and how I was using it.

In learning to study myself in relationship to the rising and the setting of the sun, I realize I was allowing myself a new way of relating to Creator and Creation—a relationship to the sun. As I was learning to study the sun and how it felt to write at different times of the day, week, month, and year, I was very sensitive—and I was becoming increasingly more aware of my sensitivity. In becoming aware of and exploring my sensitivity, I began to study the impact writing was having on my being in relationship with the people closest to me.

I felt sensitive in the sense of edginess or feeling irritable. As I currently write these words, I realize I was easily agitated back then. It was hard for me to be with too many thoughts or feelings, if I was not able to express myself—to express the thoughts and feelings I was living with and experiencing. When I finally allowed myself space and time for writing, and the meditation that came along with it, I could feel myself chang-ing with each sentence I wrote. I could hear myself growing with insights about life and living I had never considered before now. It felt amazing to be sitting in the newness of creativity.

I was learning to allow myself to see the gift in allowing the writing to teach me how to create space to calm my mind and to have ease in the present. I was learning how to be in tune with myself and to allow what wanted to come through, to come through. I wanted to know myself and I wanted to know my purpose and function in relationship to my family, community, and this society. I was determined to have the practice of *creating a space for presence* teach me how to be anchored and centered. So, I found myself sitting with myself and with the questions I had gained in my journey. I learned to value the questions as they came through, because the questions were actually statements and teachings wanting to be revealed through my life experiences.

In all the gifts I was discovering, I also found myself resenting the voice I was discovering. I was resenting how the voice sounded and I resented the places it took me. I realized I was at war with myself. I could see the active reality of living with a psychological mindset of self-hatred and self-defeat expressed by Dr. Amos N. Wilson (2019). If peace was going to be present, I would have to learn to live with myself. I would have to learn to love the voice I was given—this was part of the reason I was creating the space to be present with myself. I was learning how to love myself.

In learning how to love myself, I was learning to love the presence of the Creator and Creation in my life—including creation reflected through the people closest to me. This to me is the true meaning of *tezet*—to see the divine presence in the people closest to me. Seeing the divine presence in the people closest to me taught me to know my own divinity. *Tezet* starts and ends in the presence we share with one another. Seba Ahmad writes in *Time Dimensions and Community Development,* "The African believes that the person is shaped in community; one is not born 'human' but becomes 'human' through community" (Azzahir 2001: 120). Community makes you human and it is within community we discover the divinity of being and becoming human beings.

In being present with myself, I sit with the knowledge I feel is calling and pulling me to be present. I am sitting with the lifeforce energy that called my life into being on the planet. The pull I felt, to be at peace as a human being, is as much a part of the pull a flower feels to be the beauty it is called to be as it rises out of the dirt. As I sat with myself my desire was to know I had something of value and something beautiful inside. As I wrote, the more I wanted to write. The more I wrote the freer I felt. The freer I felt, the closer I grew in my family and community connections. I wanted to write more because I wanted the teachings that had survived my life experiences to live on. I was recognizing and acknowledging these feelings in the moment and the knowledge expressed is still present in me as I express today.

In the years since I first started with the practice of *creating a space for presence,* I have discovered peace has become a choice I have to make on a conscious level. *Who are you and what does your presence mean to the function of the cosmos? Who are your people and what do you all have to teach the world about being and becoming human beings?* These questions have grown out of the early study of myself and my people's knowledge. One of the most important lessons I have learned from life is, in order to see transformation in our lives we are required to open our hearts and minds to our ability to see transformation within ourselves. In a very real and grounded way, we have to see what we are being and becoming at the same time—we have to be willing to see someone new in the mirror of life as we study ourselves.

I have also had to learn openness. Openness has taught me to see things in myself others can't see. Being open has given me access to seeing the divine in the world around me, and because I can see the divinity in the world around me, I can see it in myself. I see how life is a reflection of Creation because I was open to the idea speaking to me. I had to become open to the transitions and intersections of being with myself. I had to become open to seeing the potential in myself. Seeing the potential in myself is what gives me the ability to see potential in other people. In being open to the atum (potential) within, I could see the potential for openness in myself and the potential to be open with those closest to me.

In studying myself in this way, I have become grateful for the many interactions that allowed me to see how the divine is functioning through me and around me. Each of the interactions I have in the world allow me to continue my journey towards developing and acknowledging the peace and love I have within myself. I have discovered the process of transformation, being and becoming at peace with myself, is what gives me the capacity to be at peace with the world around me. This journey is what gives me the capacity to allow myself to become who I am called to be.

In sharing these first thoughts of love, peace, and acceptance of myself, I pray they are gifts to whoever may come across them—the process of producing this knowledge has been edifying. I am sharing these words because I am acknowledging my own need for self-affirmation, self-acceptance, and the practice of allowing myself to express these needs for myself. I am learning to sit with myself and accept I have knowledge in order to see we all have internal knowledge that must be acknowledged and expressed. I am learning to accept I can be in alignment with the Self. I have learned to see and know myself more as a human being. I have learned *being* and *becoming* are the basic states of what it means to be consciously centered in your own life and in the interactions, we have with the divine.

The process of becoming and being tezet is teaching me to develop an understanding of myself as an eternal aspect of the cosmos. I am learning to see myself as a reflection of the divine in Creation. I am learning to sit with the truth of who I am as a human being. I am on the journey that allows me to be present in each moment of my life. In being present in each moment of life, I can create a life of peace, clarity, and calmness. When I choose to create space for peace, clarity, and calmness, I can stay on my path and live in the truth of my own life's experiences. In being and becoming in alignment with the Self, I recognize my life does not have to impede on the movements of others. I am still learning to be still in moments of disruption. The freedom of life is in our ability to be present, conscious, and active as we witness our own transformations.

Tezet is self as a reflection of
the Divine Presence in Creation.

Creating a Space for Presence

Being and Becoming Tezet:
Affirmations and Allowances

This is a self-study journal. It is a journal I initially created for myself as a set of affirmations and allowances to guide my writing time. The six sentences I talk about in the introduction are integral to how I have developed my personal approach to self-study, which I call the practice of *creating a space for presence.* In the practice of writing, I asked myself to express affirmations and allowances that would allow me to see myself as a divine presence in Creation.

This journal and practice is for anyone who is in search of peace, clarity, and calmness. If this resonates with you, know this self-study is being offered to you in this moment, as a guide towards your own Khepra journey—for you to define the truth and wisdom in your own life experiences. Each day, create a time, place, and space for yourself to have at least thirty minutes of time to write and reflect. If thirty minutes is too much time to be with your thoughts for the first time, maybe start with ten-minute intervals and work your way towards thirty minutes over time.

The following are some tips for you to create space for affirmations and allowances, as you work toward the process of learning to see yourself as the being and becoming of the divine presence in Creation:

1. Allow yourself to have an open heart.

2. Allow yourself to take it slow and do not push or force the words.

3. Allow yourself to relax into the sentences as they come through.

4. Allow yourself to be at ease, no matter what comes through—you are allowing yourself to discover new parts of yourself.

5. Allow yourself to value what comes through as a teaching for you and for those closest to you.

6. Allow yourself to realize, in writing, you are overcoming the person you have lived as, and becoming the human being you are being called to become.

I think each day can be beautiful when we allow ourselves to create beauty. Each day, as you begin *creating a space for presence*, use the writing in this self-study to help you create space for your very own process to emerge. Each day, allow yourself to find encouragement from within—this is a teaching from my mother. She would say to me often, "Encourage yourself because the world is not going to encourage you."

Allow your words to teach you how to dream of a better state of being. Allow the process of studying your own heart to guide you into closer, more intimate relationships with the people closest to you. In your creating a space for presence, allow yourself to become aware of your ability to allow yourself to have a life beyond whatever the struggle is—no matter if it is the pain, or the suffering, or the sadness that lives within the anger and rage we have to potential to carry. The practice of *creating a space for presence* is about allowing yourself to see yourself as a divine reflection of Creation, by facing life—and life starts with you.

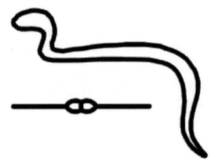

Tez is the word for the Self or
the innermost core of being.

Being Truth

Being and Becoming Tezet:
Affirmations and Allowances

Allow yourself to begin to consciously seek peace in your life and living. It is in the consciousness of your personal peace you will become conscious you are not the only person seeking peace. Allow your feelings to direct you back to peace. Allow yourself to become conscious in confronting discord with silence. Allow yourself to realize when other people appear to be in opposition to your harmony and create space to be in the presence of your own peace. Allow the Self to be present for people to see.

⮜ *Tezet 1*

Allow yourself to be present in your closest relationships. Allow yourself to give love as a peace offering. Allow yourself to be aware that truth presents itself through your ability to be honest with yourself. Allow yourself to choose to live in a way that acknowledges the importance of truth in living. Allow yourself to respond to things in ways that demonstrate you are consciously aware that you are responsible for your path and journey. Allow yourself to accept truth and begin to discover the consciousness of who you are.

⮜ *Tezet 2*

Be mindful to walk your path of being and becoming with a consciousness of a life anchored in balance. As you begin to walk with balance allow yourself to discover how you are the keeper of your peace. As a human being, you will discover you are responsible for the ways you live your life. Allow yourself to realize you are accountable for making sense of the encounters you have with other people and how those encounters impact the way you decide to live your life. Allow your peace to be an internal beacon that calls you to be ever mindful of being present and conscious of yourself as symbol of the Creator. In becoming conscious of your peace, do not allow yourself to be distracted from your peace.

❧ *Tezet 3*

Be mindful of your being as you reflect on stability for yourself and learn to live in the harmony of being present with your people. Allow yourself to be conscious of your call to be peace-filled. Allow yourself to grow into the Self. As you grow into yourself, be willing to create space to allow other people the same space to grow. Allow yourself to realize growth is a birthplace that develops as the insight of the Self develops. Allow yourself to realize inner sight is the key to living in peace with yourself and the people closest to you.

❧ *Tezet 4*

Remember to sense, see, and feel the potential in yourself and in other people. Allow the potential of your being and becoming to encourage you in your process of being at peace. Be mindful to give attention to how you respond and react to the circumstances surrounding your life and living. Allow yourself to realize your reactions and responses are opportunities to realize who you are being and what you can become. Allow yourself to speak truth to yourself about how you want to engage in your life and living. Allow yourself to become mindful of how your moods and feelings impact the relationships with the people closest to you.

◈ *Tezet 5*

Allow yourself to create space to give into living in the fullness of the Self. Allow the Self to speak for you and you will learn to be present and active in your living. Allow yourself to take time to live well. Allow yourself to become mindful of not attempting to convince other people of your being or becoming. Allow yourself to be light and to allow the Self to be reflected through your life and living. Allow yourself to become aware the truth does not have to be understood through conflict.

◈ *Tezet 6*

Allow yourself to realize the knowledge of yourself is demonstrated in how you are being and becoming. As you are becoming conscious of your life and living, apply your will toward the knowledge you are gaining. Allow yourself to become mindful of offering the world around you an authentic reflection of what you are working to become. Remember you are peace. Allow yourself to realize the strength of your peace. Allow yourself to see your peace is strong as you work to offer a clear reflection of being called into being.

◈ *Tezet 7*

As you become conscious of your process of life and living, anchor your life in transformation, being, and becoming. Allow yourself to realize as a human being, you reflect what the Creator and Creation are attempting to reflect through your life and living. Allow yourself to look at the world around you and look into your life as a process of being and becoming. Allow yourself to see how you think about yourself and your people. Allow yourself to see how you see yourself in relationship to the Creator, Creation, and the divine. Allow yourself to become conscious of what you might have missed before now.

∽ *Tezet 8*

As you become conscious of yourself, allow yourself to realize when you are missing the purpose of the lessons your life is attempting to reveal to you. Allow yourself to become aware you are receiving images and creating thought connected to the Creator and Creation. Allow yourself to uncover the secret and sacred nature present in your being and becoming. As you become conscious of this divine relationship to the All, allow yourself to realize you are revealing your creation story. Allow yourself to become grateful for all you have been given in life. Allow yourself to be mindful of your thinking and your creations.

∽ *Tezet 9*

As you begin to consider your heart as a guiding principle in your becoming, do not buy into the critics of the world. Do not allow yourself to doubt your ability to experience the presence of the divine spirit in Creation. Do not allow yourself to approach the intersections of your being and becoming with skepticism. Do not allow yourself to accept doubt as your approach to life and living. Allow yourself to realize you are learning to see the world with fresh eyes and renewed vision. Allow yourself to begin to see cynicism as judgment.

◆ *Tezet 10*

As you grow in confidence, allow yourself to observe the world with truth in order to find harmony. Allow yourself to begin to look at the world from the inside out; do not doubt the truth you are discovering in your own strength. Allow yourself to discover the delightful aspect of who you are and what you are being and becoming. As you become conscious of yourself as a reflection of Creation, realize your spirit is not weak, fragile, or easily broken. In your becoming conscious of yourself as a human being, begin to see yourself as an expression of strength and truth. Allow yourself to begin to see yourself as a part of Creation and eternally present in the heart of the Creator.

◆ *Tezet 11*

As you grow into the human being you are being called to be, imagine you are co-creating with other people as an offering of the collective knowledge your people have about being and becoming. Allow yourself to seek newness in every moment of your being and becoming. Allow yourself to discover the strength behind the wisdom you carry inside. Allow the strength of your wisdom to flow through you. Allow yourself to live in the strength of being connected to the Creator as you consider the path of your being and becoming. Allow yourself to take time to become consciously aware of how amazingly strong you are.

≈ *Tezet 12*

Allow the resilience of your spirit to be revealed in the way you live your life. Allow yourself to let go of the pains you have experienced and allow yourself to grow from the nutrients of having the wisdom given to you from the process of living. Allow yourself to take time to see past the images you are bombarded with from the outside world. Allow yourself to create space to be astonished by what you learn about who you are in your being and becoming. Allow yourself to become conscious of your spirit as truthful, courageous, and confident. Allow yourself to become conscious of yourself as a warrior for Creation as you learn to see the world through the eyes of the Creator.

≈ *Tezet 13*

Allow yourself to become aware there will be times when you will question what you see in yourself. Allow yourself to move through life knowing who you are. Realize the questions you are discovering are guiding you toward what you have been called to do. Allow yourself to be interested in all the possibilities and opportunities you will discover as you give into the process of your being and becoming. Allow your spirit to be present. Allow your spirit to be vibrant and warm. Allow yourself to create space to be present with your feelings of confidence.

≈ *Tezet 14*

Allow yourself to become comfortable with all the aspects of yourself you are uncovering as you allow yourself to contemplate your strength. In your becoming conscious of your confidence, give yourself permission to stand in the strength of the truth you are discovering. In your becoming, when you encounter difficulties, allow the strength you have discovered to give you sight beyond the challenges of life and living. Allow yourself to become conscious of the courage you are gaining as you create a vision for your life from the knowledge of your experiences. Allow yourself to see the truth of what you and your people have endured to be present on the planet. In your becoming, be aware of your endurance and release yourself from distractions that might keep you away from seeing the Self.

∽ *Tezet 15*

Allow yourself to become conscious of yourself as being enduring and resilient. Allow your endurance and adaptability to be present throughout the process of being with life and living. As you become aware of your resilience, become conscious of your ability to walk without stumbling over your past. Allow yourself to be ever present with the wisdom that has come from your life and living. Allow yourself to become conscious as you stand in assurance with your own process. Allow yourself to realize you are more than the images you are receiving from beyond yourself.

∽ *Tezet 16*

Becoming
Strength

Being and Becoming Tezet:
Affirmations and Allowances

Allow yourself to become conscious of how you question yourself about the best way to live. Allow yourself to become aware
you have to stand and live with the strength at your core. As you
stand with the strength of the Creator's voice, be mindful to
choose being at peace and ease. Allow yourself to comfortably
approach moments that may appear mundane—realizing these
moments are of your creation. Allow yourself to become consciously aware you have the ability to see beyond routine and
rote tasks of life by realizing rituals are sacred processes. Allow
yourself to see how you are created and what you are creating
through your life—and how you are living in relationship to the
divine in Creation.

∿ *Tezet 17*

Allow yourself to become aware of what has gone into making
you the person you reflect back to Creation, and the people
closest you. Allow yourself to become conscious of how you
can give birth to peace, ease, and freedom in your life. Allow
yourself to travel toward freedom by being open to experiencing the truth of what is in front you. As you become aware of
your ability to have a presence of peace, allow yourself to move
through your life and living with a settled heart and mind. Give
yourself permission to pursue clarity and calmness through
the practice of being present with the Self. Allow yourself to
realize, from a clear mind, you will encounter amazing aspects
of yourself.

∿ *Tezet 18*

Allow the perspective of yourself to renew and refresh how you are being and what you are becoming. Allow yourself to become aware your life is a gift made available to you each moment you are living. Allow yourself to become conscious of the presence of unimaginable moments of peace and ease in your life. Allow yourself to find comfort in knowing you are more than the routines of your daily life. Allow your freedom to be an expression of your ability to create peace through the ritualizing of the mundane. Allow yourself to accept the moments of serenity you have created for yourself as opportunities to discover the Self.

∽ *Tezet 19*

Give yourself permission to demonstrate the process of your transformation through being and becoming. Allow yourself to find the balance that will move you beyond simply living. Allow yourself the space to live freely. Allow yourself to discover what it means to become conscious of your understandings and experiences of the world. Allow Creation to show you the strength of your potential. Become conscious of seeking understanding to become conscious of the Self.

∽ *Tezet 20*

Ankh is the word for life and mirror.

Being Alive

Being and Becoming Tezet:
Affirmations and Allowances

Allow yourself to create spaces filled with opportunities to deeply develop the meaning of the Self. Allow yourself to understand the purpose of your journey. Allow yourself to indulge in discovering yourself. Give yourself permission to find meaning that allows you to connect with the present. Allow yourself to create freedom through the ways you practice acceptance of yourself. Allow yourself to become conscious of knowing you are not a random part of immateriality.

∽ *Tezet 21*

Allow yourself to realize your connection to other people has purpose. Allow yourself to seek understanding in what connects you and move toward your own authority to be. Become conscious of the realization only you can give life to your freedoms. Uncover the charm in your daily life. Realize you are a part of more than an isolated self. You are connected to other people through love.

∽ *Tezet 22*

Allow yourself to give life to something more than steps in a day. Allow yourself to know with certainty, your journey has purpose. Allow yourself to have a conscious realization of being intentional in your efforts to be understanding towards other people. Allow yourself to move through your life and living with intention and be resolved with your ways of being. Allow yourself to see the meaning and purpose your journey is expressing through you. Allow yourself to discover your ability to have peace and understanding as meaning and purpose reveals themselves to you.

∽ Tezet 23

Begin to allow new ways of being and becoming to be expressed through your presence. Allow yourself to imagine and discover what your life is becoming through your being. Allow yourself to be mindful of all the possibilities on your journey. Allow yourself to see how each moment of life can create enlightenment and understanding. Allow yourself to be intentional about not living too far into your future to maintain consciousness of your presence and the presence of your people. Allow yourself to become conscious of how, in being present in your moments of consciousness, you can demonstrate the presence of freedom.

∽ Tezet 24

In your being, allow yourself to see peace in your moments, becoming conscious of having moments of consciousness. Allow yourself to become conscious of the messages your path is offering you. In your becoming, allow yourself to realize joy is created by you being true to yourself. Allow yourself to take charge of discovering and knowing yourself. Allow yourself to see the consciousness of knowledge in becoming yourself. Allow yourself to take full advantage of realizing what you have not realized before.

∽ Tezet 25

In your becoming, allow yourself to set aside any preconceived ideas about who you are or what you are becoming. Only allow yourself to see what truth your moments of consciousness are offering to you. Allow yourself to realize what you are learning as your becoming unfolds. Allow yourself to see the freedom in what you are choosing for yourself. Allow what is originally inside of you, to show itself to you. Allow yourself to realize the meaning you have created in becoming.

◈ *Tezet 26*

Allow yourself to realize the meaning in your being called to the planet. Allow yourself to be in the presence of the deepest part of yourself. Allow yourself to be understanding of your-self in each moment of becoming conscious of yourself. Allow yourself to create space and presence for the understanding you have gained for your purpose. Allow yourself to be renewed by moments of understanding. Allow yourself to see the clarity of freedom as you realize the peace of sitting and seeing yourself in the light of day.

◈ *Tezet 27*

Becoming
Understanding

Being and Becoming Tezet:
Affirmations and Allowances

Allow yourself to listen to the lessons and stories being revealed
through your life and living. Allow yourself to become conscious
of listening to your voice as you tell the story attached to your
ways of being. Allow yourself to see the brilliance of being revealed in you and in other human beings. Allow your life story
to be an example of your commitment to being and becoming
what the Creator has called you to be. Allow yourself to realize
you have the ability to transform. Allow your understanding of
being human to reveal your brilliance.

◆ *Tezet 28*

Allow yourself to be refreshed in the presence of yourself. As
you are becoming conscious of yourself as a human being,
share the fruits of your becoming with the people closest to you.
Allow yourself the consciousness to create space to share the
stories of where your life and living has taken you. Allow yourself the consciousness to create space to take time to visualize
where you want to go. Allow yourself to realize you are gifted
with the ability to have a deeper understanding of the present
and the presence of being. Allow yourself to realize a sense of
renewal in being who you are called to be.

◆ *Tezet 29*

In your becoming, allow yourself to discover the wonder of
who and what your Ancestors are being and becoming in you.
Allow yourself the consciousness to create space to explore the
possibility of what your Ancestors have gifted to you. Allow
yourself to realize what you are being and becoming as you dis-

cover the essence of being you. Allow yourself to create space to explore the story of your becoming. Be mindful of the ways you commit yourself to being. Allow yourself to be renewed in what you are revealing in yourself.

≪ *Tezet 30*

In your becoming, allow yourself to take time to recall all you are becoming. Allow yourself to realize what you have discovered is called life. Allow yourself to create moments to pay attention to how you have assured yourself throughout your journey of discovery. Allow yourself to become conscious of giving your attention to the practices and disciplines that allow your spirit to feel refreshed and renewed. Allow yourself to become conscious of walking with principled steps. Allow yourself to honor all your obligations as you realize the life you have created for yourself.

≪ *Tezet 31*

As you become conscious of your voice, be intentional with the words you use about where you are headed. Allow yourself to be generously free. Allow yourself to take time to reflect on your commitment to yourself. Allow yourself to live with empathy as an expression of life. Allow yourself to become consciously aware of how you practice empathy. Allow yourself to share the gift of empathy within.

≪ *Tezet 32*

Allow yourself to discover what you will live passionately for. As you become conscious of the Self, allow yourself to realize your value and purpose as you tune into your gifts. Allow yourself to share your life experiences as you study the impact of being conscious of yourself as a human being. Allow yourself to realize empathy is a divine expression of being fully human. Allow yourself to realize all human beings are seeking ways of renewal in the evolutions and revolutions of life and living. Allow yourself to be open to seeing yourself in a new light.

∾ *Tezet 33*

Allow your ideal life to be reflected to you. As you move through life, allow yourself to be empathetic in your interactions and reactions with other people. Allow yourself to be filled with an ever-present sense of growth and renewal. Allow yourself to sit with the ease of realizing there is no other likeness the same as yours. Allow yourself to consider being true to yourself. As you become conscious of your ability to create the life you desire, allow yourself to imagine a life of renewed joy.

∾ *Tezet 34*

Being Joyful

Being and Becoming Tezet:

Affirmations and Allowances

Live life as though you walk in sunshine. Take every opportunity to see joy. Make being you the brightest part of your every moment. Live so the world will know freedom is real. Enter your path being conscious of the joy you can create. Allow yourself to accept the experience of feeling joy.

&ossh; *Tezet 35*

Allow your feelings to be delightful. Remember joy in the presence of being. Of all the feelings you will encounter, be sure to embrace joy. Allow the vibrancy of joy to be present for you and presenced through you. Be warm and experience the peace of joy. Allow yourself to realize joy is a necessity in the presence of being.

&ossh; *Tezet 36*

In this life you will have many feelings—embrace the presence of joy. Know joy is real despite how elusive it may feel. Joy is a reminder of the lightness of being. Joy is the birthplace of hope. As you journey on your path, be mindful to collect seeds of hope. Allow joy to remind you of your peace.

&ossh; *Tezet 37*

Face doubt with courage and freedom. Remember you have collected hope and the fruits of your potential for moments of doubt. Allow the accomplishments of your being to be the seeds of hope. Allow the demonstration of hope to be a gratifying experience. Protect your joy and allow it to create presence. Joy is easily squandered when we are only attempting to become conscious of happiness.

❧ *Tezet 38*

Do not allow other people to disrupt the presence of your peace. Allow potential disruptions to guide you closer to your desired presence of peace. Do not allow external pressures to disrupt your experience of peace. Remind yourself of how precious joy and peace are to you. Remember how you have learned to allow potential disruptions to pass. Joy complements and harmonizes sorrow.

❧ *Tezet 39*

Each moment is valuable. As you are becoming, be mindful of your peace. Learn who you are. Notice how it feels to settle into your joy. Be mindful of self. Joy and delight will teach you to know you are resilient.

❧ *Tezet 40*

Treasure your joy. Be joyful and journey with optimism. Know you are an expression of the life you seek. Allow joy to flow through every moment possible. Remember at the core of each moment there is peace. Your acceptance of peace creates space for freedom and joy.

❧ *Tezet 41*

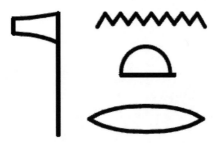

Neter is the word meaning Divine.

Becoming Free

Being and Becoming Tezet:
Affirmations and Allowances

Recall your favorite tree and see it as a symbol of freedom. Imagine you are sitting beneath it. Allow your mind to wonder why you have been chosen to become. Wonder without end, until you are at peace with yourself. Continue being and becoming. Contemplate and consider your being and discover freedom.

✦ *Tezet 42*

Cherish moments of freedom. Take time to see what these moments create for you. Realize you must take purpose and intention with you as you journey toward freedom. Take moments to breathe in life and be in the presence of freedom. When you pause, take in the process your freedom has created for you. Seeing the process is one of the greatest gifts of your being and becoming.

✦ *Tezet 43*

Realize freedom in every step you take. Allow your life to become a symbol of the freedom you have chosen. Take the journey in front of you freely and without fear or doubt. Allow yourself to feel free to refresh often. Allow your spirit to be recharged as you realize your gains. Allow the process to guide you to realize what you are gaining in your being and becoming.

✦ *Tezet 44*

Freedom will always guide you toward the Self. Allow your feelings to guide you closer to peace. Offer tears as a tribute to your persistence and determination. Know your peace comes from a place called freedom. You can shoulder all aspects of your becoming. Remember to be at peace as you learn to live in balance with yourself.

❧ *Tezet 45*

Seek balance and be free. You are free. Create whatever you choose and be honest with yourself. Freely create freedom for yourself and those closest to you. Achieve self-awareness by being and becoming. Value your freedom, it is a gift of the spirit.

❧ *Tezet 46*

Paint boldly and produce reflective images. Do not allow anything to limit the imagination. Do not allow doubt to create limitations for you. Allow your heart to produce the images you desire to create. Allow the images you create to bring you to peace. Allow your works to give you access to greater peace and be humble in your process.

❧ *Tezet 47*

Allow your life to teach you how to practice humility. As you become aware of your own understanding, allow other people the space to become aware of their understanding. Be present with the greatest peace. The greatest peace lives in turning your pain and suffering into knowledge. Give life to your ability to be healed. Discover your vision.

❧ *Tezet 48*

Hold your feelings long enough for them to show you truth. Freedom is present in every truth we face. Allow yourself to experience freedom in your relationships as you work toward healing. Know your reflections are gifts for you and for those closest to you. Smile in moments of realized growth. Moments of growth are openings into the becoming of the Self.

≪ *Tezet 49*

Walk in the fullness of your freedom. Discover the enlightenment in being and becoming the Self. Know you are reflecting the path of your own transformation. As you journey toward the Self, you will uncover discomfort and joy. Do not approach feelings with judgment. Know anxiety does not allow you to create freedom; rise above worry and fear.

≪ *Tezet 50*

Experience moments of freedom with gratitude. Seek peace in growth and becoming. As you journey, remember you are a gift to Creation. The gift is present in you and the images you create. Remember, your creations are reflections of your heart. Know you are free to continue your becoming.

≪ *Tezet 51*

Find peace in knowing you are created to reflect Creation. Take the steps on your path with a light heart. You are becoming the peace you are seeking in your process. Allow your becoming to presence the truth of your lived experience. Begin to experience the truth of the transformation. Be free to become what you have been created to be.

≪ *Tezet 52*

Being
Knowledge

Being and Becoming Tezet:

Affirmations and Allowances

Find your ability to know the way you live. Life is an amazing opportunity. Look for moments to give to yourself. Create knowledge to teach yourself to grow faith. Allow yourself to create space to see how hope produces knowledge. Producing the knowledge of yourself takes time and discipline.

◈ *Tezet 53*

Learn to live with certainty and knowing. Do not hide yourself. Hoping to be free is not freedom. Be mindful of your freedom and choose it. Live a life free of fear. See all the possibilities you have now given yourself.

◈ *Tezet 54*

Trust in what you know and in what you are learning about yourself. Know you have all you need to become who you are. Stand in the knowledge of your being. Allow peace into your heart, mind, body, and spirit. Live in the presence of the love you are sharing. If you do not love yourself, pause and consider what it means to love who you are.

◈ *Tezet 55*

Do not live life with suffering and call it love. Authentic love comes from acceptance of yourself. Settle into loving yourself. Discover the relationship between love and knowledge. Allow yourself to see all of the possibilities in your growth. Come alive with your knowledge you are producing for yourself.

◈ *Tezet 56*

Love yourself and know you are complete. Acceptance of yourself is freedom. Practice the art of self-love. Discipline is allowing yourself to become. There is no need to hide who you are. See yourself for who you are.

∾ *Tezet 57*

Accept yourself. You are a reflection of transformation. Become aware of the knowledge held in being transformed. See the value in developing yourself. Be mindful of yourself when you give. See the potential in the ability to grow freedom.

∾ *Tezet 58*

Know your potential. Allow yourself to see the potential in the ability to love yourself. Share the knowledge of your becoming in the way you live. Be selfless in knowing and learning yourself. Loving yourself increases your ability to share love with other people. Love who you are.

∾ *Tezet 59*

AFRICAN PARADIGM OF KNOWLEDGE
SPIRITUALITY – SYMBOL – MYTHOS – HARMONIUM

Being Original

Being and Becoming Tezet:
Affirmations and Allowances

Be original; see how much you understand about life. Be mindful of the trees as you travel. In your becoming, be aware of how your tree reflects you. See how the branches shift and sway with the wind. Enjoy the way the leaves give way and hold. See yourself reflected and know freedom.

✺ *Tezet 60*

Be curious about how unique you are. Be mindful of how you are created. Realize, like all beings, you have value simply in the presence of your being. Allow joy to be present in your becoming. Imagine and realize you are amazing. You are as beautiful as any leaf on any tree.

✺ *Tezet 61*

You are learning to depend on your inner being in your becoming. Become, knowing all of humanity is seeking sight. Discover you are wonderful in your own way. You are brilliant. Allow yourself to understand the brilliance emanating from within. Engage with the reality of the divine.

✺ *Tezet 62*

Allow yourself the freedom to be who you are being called to become. Give to the world by being exceptional in all your ways of being. Each human being is learning to know their calling in life. Settle into the calling of your being. You are in the process of discovering your own completeness. See everyone in their being and becoming, and celebrate in the freedom they are sharing.

✺ *Tezet 63*

There are no limits in your ability to manifest freedom. Being free is not based on your interactions with other people. Freedom is a measure of your own heart. When you uncover the freedom within, you will realize you are growing. See your growth as an eternal process of being and becoming. Your creativity will grow when you begin to grow with other people. You are able to see Creation and experience the Creator.

∽ Tezet 64

See freedom as a conscious state of being and becoming. Be mindful of the role conscious freedom plays in your life. Give yourself permission to delight in the consciousness of who you are. Be completely interested in the difference and the sameness you discover between you and other people. Be mindful of how you respond to the variations in peace you discover; remember stillness. Learn to see beyond the separation between you and other people.

∽ Tezet 65

Allow other people to be who they are; this is an expression of your sharing of freedom. Your role is not to offer judgment, only presence and empathy. Create space for self-growth in order for the growth of other people to be visible. Humanity will evolve in the evolutions of your relationships. Be free to delight in the distinctiveness of being who you are called to be. Be mindful of how you create connection and disconnection.

∽ Tezet 66

See how you have moved past discontent in your life. Realize the consciousness of your originality. See the complementary aspects of who you are and how visible they are in the world around you. See your reflection in other people and realize how beautiful we are as human beings. Travel with a liberated realization of your being and becoming. Be present in your consciousness, and as you journey, know your potential is infinite.

∿ *Tezet 67*

Becoming Eternal

Being and Becoming Tezet:
Affirmations and Allowances

Being is realizing life and living are eternal processes of being and becoming. In becoming conscious of your life and living, you will release some of your own convictions. Allow the freest reality to speak its truth to you. Free yourself from things that limit your ability to see the eternal. In considering the eternal, do not attach yourself to arrogance. Be conscious of humility and be direct.

෴ *Tezet 68*

Being in the presence of other people can feel overwhelming. See your peace as anchored in eternity. Your ability to produce peace is your greatest strength. The ability to feel allows you to give life to a renewed consciousness of your peace. You are feeling. See your feelings as a part of Creation's design for you to be mindful of your realization of peace.

෴ *Tezet 69*

Each finite moment is an ending and a beginning. Allow yourself to be transformed by what each of your moments leave with you. Transformation is a process that gives life to the eternal. Be mindful to celebrate each moment in the realization of the eternal. Allow yourself to give into the opportunity to become mindful of something amazing. See the eternal in the presence of other people's being and becoming.

෴ *Tezet 70*

Allow the moments of being to teach you how to smile as you become conscious of your individuated self. Allow yourself to give into the acceptance of who you are and the value of your presence. You are not asking permission to be or to become the Self. In eternity, you have been known and seen forever. See the connections of affirmations as elements Creation is offering you toward your being and becoming. See what you are connected to.

꙳ *Tezet 71*

See how your connections are attached to eternity. Each person you come into contact with has purpose. Discover who and what you are eternally connected to. See the truth in the connections you share with the eternal. Visit and recreate past moments to remind you of your growth. Allow this process to teach you the value of symmetry.

꙳ *Tezet 72*

Take in the mental images around you and see the contrast in the image of yourself as eternal. Consider the value of the discovering the reflection of your own being and becoming one with the eternal. Learn from the insights you have been given from living. Consider how remarkable discovering the gift behind life and living is. See yourself living in all time. You are past and present. See yourself as future.

꙳ *Tezet 73*

Do not choose to allow your thoughts to hold you prisoner. To choose to be confined by your thoughts is unreasonable and will only create misery. Release the need to fight your thoughts as you are becoming. Create space to study your thoughts and what creates the patterns of your thinking. Do not deny yourself life. Do not allow yourself to be caught up in the misery of the mundane.

∾ *Tezet 74*

See yourself and allow the wonder of who are to shine through. Seeing the brevity of life gives us access to the consciousness of moments as finite. Consider the finite as a path toward the consciousness of the eternal. Allow your consciousness of the eternal to encourage you to live authentically free. Accept your ability to imagine and manifest space and time to be in the presence of the eternal. Create space for yourself to give birth to visions of peace for your life.

∾ *Tezet 75*

Allow yourself to see your freedom as intrinsic and natural. Allow space for the eternal to live through your presence and being. Be mindful of the desire to live excessively. Be mindful of how you are consciously becoming the Self. Give life to the eternal as you become conscious of your birth and rebirth. Learn to accept the fullness of who you are in yourself.

∾ *Tezet 76*

Being Accepting

Being and Becoming Tezet:
Affirmations and Allowances

Sharing your journey with other people allows you to practice acceptance of yourself. Learn your path will cross with others. Share your path with those closest to you. Create home with your family and friends. Allow yourself to accept how your relationships are supporting your becoming. The road ahead of you is the path inside of you.

❧ *Tezet 77*

Successes and disappointments teach us acceptance. Understand your path. Overcome any obstacle you encounter. Accept your story. Know the people walking with you are teaching you how to be. In order to be, you have to allow yourself to accept yourself.

❧ *Tezet 78*

See the importance of your reflection. Share the best of yourself as you share space with other people. You are can never overshadow the Self. Your relationships reflect the truest images of who we are. You will learn the potential in yourself. See the relationship to acceptance in the development of yourself as you become conscious of yourself.

❧ *Tezet 79*

Developing a desire to accept yourself is motivation to become who you are called to be. Allow yourself to make sense of what your reflection is creating for you. Offer the inner vision of yourself to yourself as a part of self-acceptance. See fullness in your life as you accept the process of your becoming. Allow yourself to discover the truth of what it means to have increased sight. Acceptance allows you to know truth of what has created you.

◈ *Tezet 80*

Take note of the similarities of the branches of the trees closest to you. We are all learning to see ourselves as individuated and connected to the source of all Creation. You are a human being seeing life for what life has to offer you in accepting the process of life and living you have been given. You are rooted in freedom. Be grounded by the shared roots of the people closest to you. See the potential in accepting all the parts of yourself.

◈ *Tezet 81*

In accepting yourself you will discover you are an amazing and miraculous human being. In accepting yourself you give yourself permission to live. Allow your spirit to rise as though you are a branch reaching for the sun. Allow yourself to have more life. Your relationships to other human beings do not limit your ability to accept yourself. Your relationships give you limitless possibilities in your becoming accepting of who you are.

◈ *Tezet 82*

Find pride in your family connections and relationships. Create space to embrace who you are becoming as a complement to your family's presence. See your becoming as an addition to the branches of your family tree. Learn to accept your connection to the Ancestors. Your brilliance is a reflection of your Ancestors presence and contribution to the planet. In accepting yourself, you are contributing to the evolution of your people's being and becoming.

◈ *Tezet 83*

Allow yourself to know you contribute to the wonder of your family's contribution to humanity. Allow yourself to practice the process of self-acceptance. Allow yourself to see the time you have created for yourself to contemplate your being and becoming. Consider the relationships closest to you and allow them to teach you acceptance of yourself. Allow yourself to be astounded at the beauty you find as you discover the gift of accepting yourself and your family. Allow yourself to live in the freedom of reaching for the sun.

◈ *Tezet 84*

Be nourished by your roots and your ability to create the space for who you are being and becoming. See yourself emerging because of the acceptance of yourself. Allow yourself to be mindful of your relationship to the sun. Allow your life and living to be a source of life and living for the people closest to you. Allow yourself to contribute to the freedom we have in being connected to the soil and the sky. You are a magnificent human being.

◈ *Tezet 85*

Allow yourself to move through what you have gone through in your life and living. Allow yourself to choose the life you desire to have. Allow yourself to stand without fear and reach for the fullness of life. Do not allow fear to distract you from living a full life. Allow each moment of self-acceptance you experience, to be an opportunity to express the fullness of living freely. Allowing yourself to be distracted by fear will limit your process of being and becoming.

◈ *Tezet 86*

Allow your life to show itself to you. You have the ability to live beyond fear. You are becoming mindful of how to live without choosing fear. As you learn to accept yourself be mindful to cherish your life and know you do not have to sacrifice living. Realize your anxieties are moments of emotional awareness. Be mindful of your reaction and move into acceptance of yourself.

◈ *Tezet 87*

Accept you are created with knowledge and you are resilient. Allow yourself to accept your ability to hold on to life without ending. Accept you are complete in every aspect of your life and living. Embrace the acceptance of yourself and the insight you are being given in your being and becoming. Allow yourself to see your life is brilliant. Allow yourself to take time to pause and discover what acceptance is creating for you.

◈ *Tezet 88*

Allow the vision of accepting yourself to teach you about who you are. See yourself from different stages in your process of transformation, being, and becoming. Take time to make the meaning held in accepting the humanity within yourself. Allow yourself to discover your ability to choose self-acceptance as you learn to live better. Be mindful of your transformation in the process of life and living. Be mindful of yourself and allow yourself to take in the newness in your breath.

Tezet 89

Allow yourself to release any preconceived identities for a moment. Allow your heart to settle into the truth of who you are as you practice accepting the Self. Allow your mind to release any anxiety you are holding on to as you become aware of yourself. Step into your being and becoming with the confidence self-acceptance is offering you. As you accept yourself, value those closest to your heart. Acceptance of yourself will allow you to share love in your moments of freedom.

Tezet 90

Be mindful of allowing yourself space to experience new ways of becoming. Allow yourself to erase the remnants of what is not serving your being and becoming. Paint images that allow you to see the ways you have learned the acceptance of your freedom. Allow your heart to create visions from the moments you are present with the Self. Allow yourself to create moments of wellness and ease. Realize, in moving toward the acceptance of yourself, you are moving toward the acceptance of your freedom.

Tezet 91

Becoming Light

Being and Becoming Tezet:
Affirmations and Allowances

Allow yourself to see the paths you are choosing in practicing self-acceptance. In learning to accept yourself, you are being and becoming light. There is lightness in learning to value the role you have been given in your life and living. Allow the lightness of your being to teach you how to master yourself as you begin to practice life with a light heart. Allow yourself to begin to see what you are offering other people in your being and becoming light. Paint images that demonstrate your practice of living in the lightness of being.

≈ *Tezet 92*

Allow yourself to see you are the light in the vision being shared from your being. Allow the lightness of your being to guide you toward ways to live in your own wellness. Realize as you move toward the light inside yourself, you are moving toward the light of Creation. See yourself as a path toward Creation as you learn to create light with your being. Allow yourself to become conscious of your ability to sustain the lightness of being in your heart. As you study the light within your heart, you are becoming conscious of the light of the Creator.

≈ *Tezet 93*

Allow the light of your being to make the Self visible for you to see. Allow the light of your being to teach you to approach the challenging moments in life with ease and peace. Remember who you are and what your position in life is requiring of you as you discover the peace in being and becoming light. As you become conscious of your own light you will increase your ability to embrace the lightness of being in other people. See yourself with the knowledge to create a life for yourself. Allow yourself to become conscious of yourself as you face questions of uncertainty and doubt about the lightness of your being.

❧ *Tezet 94*

Allow yourself to become aware of the light you are discovering within yourself and the impact the discovery is having on your being and becoming. You have been gifted with the ability to give life to wonder and awe through your being. Begin to allow yourself to see how your light allows the world to feel the warmth of your being. Allow yourself to be conscious of the process of how awe and wonder to are added the world. Be mindful to appreciate the light you have been give and the complementary light you share with other people as you become conscious of yourself. Allow yourself to offer light toward the relationships you want to create as you begin to live with a light heart.

❧ *Tezet 95*

In being mindful of how you share and foster love, you will become conscious of the light you are offering to the world around you. Allow yourself to see how your light is present in all your moments of being and becoming. In learning to value your light, you will learn to create space for other people to value the light they hold inside themselves. Become conscious of how you are sharing the light of your life and living. In your consciousness of being light, you will discover the brilliance of the love you have to offer. Each of us is learning to demonstrate our practice of acceptance and gratitude through seeing newness available in the gift of holding light.

❧ *Tezet 96*

Be mindful of the way light has the ability transform your relationship with wisdom. Allow yourself to see the insight other people offer to you through the sharing of their stories. Allow your story to reflect how you have learned to lean into knowledge over fear. Allow the lightness of being to guide you towards mastery in being mindful of your choices. Allow the forces of light to guide you toward a visualization of the freedom you have available through your life and living.

❧ *Tezet 97*

In learning to master lightness remember fear is only present to orient you back to the center of your peace. Remember to take time to find quiet time for reflection. Be mindful to create space for you to study the conditions of your heart. Allow the safety you create to guide you towards peace, comfort, and ease. Allow yourself to remember the purpose of your peace is to create a conscious awareness of your relationship with the Creator and Creation. Be mindful of allowing yourself to release any impulse to ruminate in feelings of anxiety.

❧ *Tezet 98*

Be mindful of approaching your life and living with a consciousness of the light you are carrying. Being mindful of your light teaches you how to master your fears. Allow yourself to realize how your life and living are limited by fear. Learning to live with a light heart allows you to know there are other ways of living outside of stress and distress. Allow yourself to see how the ways you have been in relationship with fear and worry have worked against you. Allow yourself to become mindful of the moments in life that ask you to take time to pause and reflect.

∾ *Tezet 99*

Allow your experiences and feelings of nervousness and fear to teach you to see what creates disruption in your being of light. Allow yourself to learn how to create peace in moments that cause you to feel outside of the lightness of your being. Learn to see how knowledge of the light you carry teaches you how to be in relationship with the light of Creation. Allow yourself to know each moment of your life and living has the potential to teach you how to increase the presence of your light. Be conscious of how you are learning to love who you are in deeper ways. Allow your mind to know you are connected to the Creator at the core of your being.

∾ *Tezet 100*

By learning to live in the lightness of your being, you will discover you have the capacity to face the life in front of you. Allowing yourself to have a life anchored in knowledge teaches you to trust the experiences you are having as you move toward transformation. Allow yourself to grow freedom from the challenges you will face. Remember your reflection is light. Allow yourself to see yourself and the life you are facing is the life you are resolving inside of yourself. Allow yourself to see how you can make peace with dis-ease.

∽ *Tezet 101*

Allow yourself to create space to learn from the fullness of your life experiences. Learning to see the fullness in the lessons attached to your life and living gives you access to accepting yourself as a human being with an eternal light of being. Allow yourself to create space for other people to teach you how to be present and live in the moment. Be mindful of how you are using peace when you choose to grow your light. Allow the sun to teach you how to practice life and living. Allow yourself to accept the embrace of being an eternal being of peace-filled light.

∽ *Tezet 102*

Allow your heart to turn the difficult moments into knowledge about how to live with lightness and being. Allow your heart to turn your fear into knowledge that teaches you how to sustain your peace. Allow your heart to turn the restlessness of anxiety into the presence of calm and stillness. Allow yourself to choose knowledge of yourself as the path that allows you to have a still mind. Become conscious of how your light is an intentional part of Creation's design of who you are as a human being. Allow your light to guide you toward the purpose of your being light.

∽ *Tezet 103*

Being Intentional

Being and Becoming Tezet:
Affirmations and Allowances

Allow your thoughts of wonder to create freedom. Remember your being was created at the beginning of time. Be intentional to study what you are becoming. Allow yourself to see how wonderfully you are created. Allow yourself to be mindful of who and what you are discovering as you study yourself. Allow yourself to study the power you hold as you learn to lean into intentionality.

∽ *Tezet 104*

Remember your words are a new creation birthed from the heart of the Creator. Allow yourself to become conscious of each syllable you produce as you focus on your intention and purpose. As you take intentional steps toward seeing your humanity, remember each intention involves your ability to decide how you want to experience life and living. Allow yourself to see the clarity, vision, intention, and meaning for each decision. Meaning has the ability to create impact. Your peace radiates through each generation; live.

∽ *Tezet 105*

Allow yourself to become mindful of speaking with the intention to study your own of voice of wisdom. Allow yourself to speak with the truth rooted in harmony and peace. Allow yourself to see your capacity to focus on your intentions. Allow yourself to create space to sit with the questions that come from the experiences of your life and living. Be mindful to give your intention the same care you would give a child. Remember peace can be expressed with intention.

∽ *Tezet 106*

As you develop intention, consider the solidity and the fluidity of what you will manifest. Allow your words to give birth to moments. Be mindful of how you unburden suffering. As you learn to release suffering, allow yourself to see how you are in relationship with Creation. You are learning to see yourself at the origins of humanity.

∽ *Tezet 107*

Allow yourself to see what knowledge will be produced out of a dedication to your process of being and becoming. Allow yourself to see yourself as the draft artist. Allow your heart to give life to brilliance. Allow yourself to be committed to the truth driving you to become conscious of your life and living. Each human being is learning to understand how life is a reflection of truth. Each human being is learning to see how the Creator and Creation made each person intentionally free. In seeing the truth of who you are to the Creator and Creation, you are seeing the Self.

∽ *Tezet 108*

Allow yourself to take time and space to notice how truth offers itself to you. Allow yourself to learn to discover the skill it takes to digest, balance, and share truth. Allow the rigidity you discover in the process of becoming to teach you how to preserve your peace. Allow yourself to be intentional as you focus your consciousness on intentionally accepting the process of your own being and becoming. Allow yourself to be at peace in your being and becoming. Allow yourself to discover how feelings impact how you choose to experience life and living.

∼ *Tezet 109*

Allow yourself to always choose to love yourself and what you are becoming. Remember, sharing love is an intentionality. Be mindful of focusing on the intentionality influencing your decisions to share love. See how you are being intentional in practicing humility through deciding how to live. Allow yourself to realize you are full of purpose and vision. Allow yourself to smile as you realize how wonderful it feels to create spaces of intentionality.

∼ *Tezet 110*

Allow yourself to be intentional to witness the truest reflection being presenced through your life and living. Be intentional in witnessing the lightness of your being in relationship to other people being light. Be intentional about facing the mirror within. Allow yourself to trust the vision you see of yourself being. Allow yourself to know you are a human being. Remember, transformation is possible when you become intentional in the steps you take toward becoming conscious of yourself.

∼ *Tezet 111*

Being Being

Being and Becoming Tezet:
Affirmations and Allowances

In your being and becoming, allow yourself to see how empathy is the driving force behind your feelings. Allow yourself to learn to see how your life and living is filled with joy. In your being and becoming, allow yourself to find new ways of sharing life. Allow empathy to give you new ways to understand yourself. Allow yourself to share empathy with the people you share your life with. Allow yourself to acknowledge suffering as you become conscious of the empathy.

◈ *Tezet 112*

Allow yourself to become conscious of what it means to live in the moment. Allowing yourself to see the suffering of your life experiences will allow you to practice self-empathy. Allowing yourself to see how you engage with the presence of suffering in your life, will teach you how you engage with the suffering in the lives of other people. Allow yourself to visualize a life without suffering. Realize the ways despair forces you into suffering. Allow yourself to become conscious of despair and how it limits your ability to take steps toward your becoming.

◈ *Tezet 113*

Allow yourself to discover new ways of releasing suffering from your experiences of life and living. Allow yourself to discover new ways to share empathy for all human beings who are experiencing the process of life and living. Allow yourself to see the discipline required to move from faith to knowledge. Allow yourself to find peace in the process of knowing who you are. Allow yourself to find grounding in the knowledge you have gained from the practices of peace and empathy. Allow yourself to become conscious of your potential to remove suffering from your process of life and living.

∽ *Tezet 114*

Allow yourself to create spaces where your greatest peace can be held. Allow yourself to be confident in how you express the presence of your being and becoming. Allow yourself to see the path of suffering is only one option. Allow yourself to see how suffering as a condition impacts the process of being and becoming a human being. Allow yourself to create a path that can be shared with people who are learning to create a life of freedom. As a human being, you are learning to create a life and living from the knowledge held in your life's experiences.

∽ *Tezet 115*

Allow yourself to create a life that rises above suffering. Allow yourself to see the freedom in who you are created to be as you learn to turn your pain and suffering into knowledge. Allow yourself to make space in your life to study the pain you have experienced. In learning to rise above suffering and pain, allow yourself to see the difference between anguish and discomfort. Allow yourself to create openings for yourself to process the learning that takes place as you are becoming conscious of the Self. Allow yourself to learn how to delineate between the knowing and hoping.

∽ *Tezet 116*

Know you are able to survive the pain present in your life. Misery and anguish are at the root of the suffering around you. Allow yourself to release feelings that take away from your ability to witness your being and becoming free. Do not tolerate things that feel excessive or unnecessary. Allow yourself to become conscious of a life guided by knowledge, peace, and love. Know that grief is a difficult place to live for too long.

~ *Tezet 117*

Allow yourself to discover parts of yourself that have been underdeveloped. Life is a process of cycles and circles that can feel as though things are always changing. It is in learning to accept the support of your elders we learn to see the value of being in relationship with the cycles and circles of life. Allow yourself to support the development of other people as you allow yourself to receive support. In facing the difficulties of life, we learn to move with faith in knowing. Allow yourself to embrace the darkness that is caring for you as you are learning to move through dark places.

~ *Tezet 118*

Learning to trust your inner light requires you to see the darkness of being and becoming are one. In your life and living, you are giving birth to Creation's ability to express itself. Allow yourself to realize and know the divine in a profoundly intimate way. Allow periods of grief to teach you how to remember memories of joy, peace, and ease. Remember you have created memories to teach yourself how to survive the pain of being with grief. In learning to release the pain you have been living with, you allow yourself to be present with your inner light.

Tezet 119

Allow yourself to see how your inner child is resilient and enduring. Allow yourself to catch yourself smiling as you witness yourself in the mirror of being one with life. Allow the smiles you offer to yourself to hold thoughts of peace and self-acceptance. When you are grieving remember when you were the most loving to yourself. As you learn to grieve and mourn, allow yourself to find peace in weeping. Allow yourself to resolve pain and suffering through loving and caring for yourself.

Tezet 120

Allow yourself to find comfort knowing you are not alone in the process of your being and becoming. Allow yourself to see the magical connections your life is creating for you, as you come into being human. Allow yourself to realize how enduring the relationships you form will become. Remember to express gratitude for the people you have loved and lost during your process of being and becoming. Allow yourself to create spaces that honor the presence of the teachings from the people you have lost. Allow yourself to remember the countless moments of transformation, being, and becoming you have experienced in your life and living.

Tezet 121

It is in learning how to accept the loss of who you were that gives you permission to see what you are becoming. In your becoming, allow yourself to share tears with other people when you experience the loss of people you have cared for in life. Allow yourself to learn how to show reverence for the tears other people share with you. Allow your spirit and soul to presence peace as you share space with other human beings. Allow yourself to accept all you are, all you have experienced, and all you are becoming.

∾ *Tezet 122*

In your becoming, you will realize life is not always traveled lightly. Remember you have never lost the connection to your original strength. Your strength is connected to the Creator and Creation. Allow yourself to see the value in allowing the Self to be present. As you walk through the doors of your life, allow yourself to pause to take in what is being revealed to you. As you move through your life, allow yourself to learn how to slow down to realize your relationship to Creation and to the cosmos.

∾ *Tezet 123*

Remember to allow yourself to experience a sense of the vibrancy as you learn to live in the present. Allow yourself to notice how it feels to take in the sky. Allow yourself to see the beauty as you encounter the blending of grays and sunlight. Remember to become conscious of your breath as you take in Creation. Allow yourself to accept the time you have created to breathe consciously. Allow yourself to become conscious of how you are connected to the movement of the world around you.

✦ *Tezet 124*

Allow yourself to become conscious of how you are creating time for yourself. Allow yourself to see how you are creating time for yourself by allowing yourself space to learn how you are connected to the universe. Allow yourself to have time to sit quietly with your heart open to all Creation. Allow yourself to create space and to feel the pulse of the wind. Allow yourself to become conscious of how the wind touching your face is an affirmation of your being a human being. As you learn to be in the presence of Creation, allow yourself to be held by the presence of peace.

✦ *Tezet 125*

Allow yourself to find time to experience peace with the people you are closest to. Remember life can be surprising and amazing. Allow yourself to be prepared to experience the wonderful and amazing experiences waiting for you in your life and living. As you move through life, allow yourself the ability to experience stillness and calmness in every aspect of your being and becoming. Allow yourself to be intentional in acknowledging all the aspects of your brilliance. Allow the brilliance you realize inside of yourself, to teach you how to see the joy present in your life.

✦ *Tezet 126*

Allow yourself to see yourself as a human being who is learning to see the Self. Allow yourself to see who you are with your heart open. Allow yourself to feel how the beats in your heart flow when you are accepting of yourself. Allow yourself to create space that allows you to spend time experiencing the lightness of life and living. Allow yourself to embrace the discovery of being in time. Allow yourself to create space and time for meditation and prayer.

* *Tezet 127*

Allow your heart to guide your sight. Allow yourself the see the most beautiful aspects of your life's path. Allow yourself to notice how you have been orientated to ignore beauty. In your life and living, remember the moments that have taught you the value of space and time for stillness and quiet. In your becoming, allow yourself to experience the wonder and delight presenced in the world around you. Allow yourself to discover what you feel you have been missing and see how you lack for nothing.

* *Tezet 128*

Allow yourself to see how your imagination can take you atop beautiful mountain spaces. Allow yourself to see the light as you reflect the time you have spent being mindful of your peacefulness. Allow yourself to be still and in the present. Allow yourself to create with the visions you have been given. Allow yourself to see what you are creating with the truth. Remember what you know about other people as you discover you lack for nothing.

* *Tezet 129*

Remember to create space each day to be present with the wonder that is present in your life and living. Allow yourself to realize you have all you need. Allow yourself to create as a means of fulfilling your prayers and wishes. Allow yourself to realize it is in sharing your gifts with other people you create the path to move beyond scarcity. Allow yourself to be conscious of what creates the sense of need in your life. Create space and time to consider what your most basic necessities for life and living are.

≈ *Tezet 130*

Allow the Self to create the path toward healing yourself. Become conscious of your path as a roadmap toward your well-being. Allow your map to wellness to teach you how beautiful you are. Create space and time to become conscious of what it means to be awed by your place in life. Allow yourself to be motivated by the desire to have truth guide your life and living. Allow yourself to live with the unending vision of being in divine alignment with the Creator and Creation.

≈ *Tezet 131*

Allow your spirit to give birth to originality. Create time to consider how you are working towards fulfilling your life's mission. Allow yourself to become conscious of how you will move forward with intention and vision. Allow yourself to see how your past, and the past of your people, is the knowledge motivating you to discover the origins of who you are. It is in being present with your past you discover what has been true about who you are since your beginning. Allow yourself to unearth your true potential by being present with the truth of who you are.

∝ *Tezet 132*

It is in allowing yourself to accept the gift of knowledge you become conscious of the power you hold inside of your being. Allow yourself to become intentional in remembering peace as you learn to care for yourself and the people closest to you. Allow yourself to spend time overcoming the barriers that distract you from focusing on your growth. Become conscious of what it means to live in the boldness of your presence. Growing into the knowledge of who you are, is knowing you have nothing to fear in facing the truth of who you are and who you are being called to become. Allow your heart to guide your steps toward your living in the presence of who you are.

∝ *Tezet 133*

Becoming Being

Being and Becoming Tezet:
Affirmations and Allowances

Allow yourself to see how speaking without empathy can cause pain and suffering for other people. In your transformation, you are called to love yourself and other people. Allow yourself to see the power in your voice. Allow yourself to embrace the aspects of your being that want to be unleashed. Allow yourself to release excessive thoughts around the pain you have experienced to eliminate space for suffering to grow. In learning to move through discomfort, allow yourself to see how pain has the potential to change the ways you share love with other people.

❧ *Tezet 134*

In your process of transformation, allow yourself to see your expression of truth as an expression of love. Allow yourself to see how you are the presence of love for other people. Allow yourself to become conscious of when you are not being loving to yourself or other people. Allow your words to be in alignment with the ways you share love through your being. Allow yourself to see how your words and deeds are in alignment with one another. You do not have to defend what you know. Allow yourself to see how you are functioning in alignment with the Creator's love and empathy.

❧ *Tezet 135*

Allow yourself to study the potential in your harvesting the knowledge held in the process of your transformation, being, and becoming. Allow yourself to use the capacity to love yourself to teach you how to create peace for yourself and the people closest to you. Allow yourself to discover how love creates the presence of warmth and comfort. Allow yourself to realize you can transform the pain and suffering from your life and living into knowledge that will teach you ways to protect your heart. Allow yourself to soften the presence of your heart as you learn your ability to share love. Allow yourself to see who you are at your core.

∽ *Tezet 136*

Allow yourself to realize love and empathy are responses you are receiving from Creation. Allow yourself to search inwardly for peace. Allow yourself to become conscious of the love and empathy available inside of yourself. Create space and time for yourself to study the knowledge of being with other human beings. Allow yourself to see beyond the distractions attempting to convince you that you are not complete. As you are learning to see yourself as a participant in Creation, you will begin to see the Creator is everywhere.

∽ *Tezet 137*

Allow yourself to become conscious of the source of Creation that flows through you. Allow yourself to see the Creator's love is what you are being called to be. Life is not something have to beg for. Allow yourself to visualize a world where love is not something you have to ask other people for. Allow yourself to become open to receiving yourself as the presence of a love that is self-sustaining and self-fulfilling. Allow yourself to become conscious of your feelings as a source of divine truth.

∽ *Tezet 138*

Allow yourself to learn to overcome fear with knowledge and truth. Allow yourself to become conscious of your ability to master the life that has been given to you by the Creator. Allow yourself to create space and time to cultivate the intelligence of your heart as knowledge, as you go face-to-face with the unknown. In learning to see yourself as a human being, allow yourself to reveal the aspects of who you are being and becoming. Allow yourself to see your journey is an original aspect of being called into being. You are learning to see yourself as a reflection of the Creator's potential.

∽ *Tezet 139*

Allow yourself to discover the fearlessness of the universe inside of you. Allow yourself to become conscious of your ability to realize freedom within yourself. In learning to be present with the freedom of Creation, you are being asked to see the freedom being birthed in your becoming. By learning to trust the knowledge you gain from your past experiences, you will learn how competent you are in facing the difficulties of life. In learning to face the unknown, you will learn to see how the unknown can become knowable. Allow yourself to take the journey into unknown aspects of who you are to overcome the fear of what you have been called to be.

∽ *Tezet 140*

Plant seeds toward knowing the unknown aspects of yourself. Give yourself access to knowing you have light within your being. Allow yourself to develop faith in the knowledge you are gaining as you study the becoming of yourself and your people. Allow yourself to create moments to examine the power you have discovered on your path of being and becoming. Allow yourself to become conscious of how it feels to plant towards your own being and becoming. Allow yourself to accept how it feels to be conscious of becoming aware of yourself as a human being.

∽ *Tezet 141*

Allow yourself to discover the wonder in being and becoming conscious of yourself. Realize the strength at the core of your being to counter the forces of fear being promoted outside of you. Allow yourself to become conscious of the relationship between your head, heart, and consciousness. Allow yourself to realize the fearlessness that has created your presence on the planet. Be mindful of taking time to consider what is being planted in your consciousness. Allow yourself to become conscious of cultivating the known and unknown aspects of your consciousness.

∽ *Tezet 142*

Allow yourself to realize power and resilience emanate from a source that exists inside of you. Allow yourself to become conscious of how hope has the capacity to become faith, and how faith has the capacity to grow into knowledge and knowing. Allow yourself to become conscious of your will to grow beyond your current state of consciousness you are experiencing. Allow yourself to realize your confidence and allow yourself to become. Remember to carry hope with you today as you rise to face the unknown aspects of your being and becoming. Allow yourself to see you are sacred and you hold the best that Creation has to offer toward our collective becoming as human beings.

∽ *Tezet 143*

See the gift of the life you have been given. With an open heart, allow yourself to discover what being present in your consciousness is showing you. Allow yourself to share the rituals and ceremonies you have discovered to support other people taking the journey into uncovering the sacred aspects of their own being and becoming. Remember, you are making conscious choices to discover more of yourself on the journey of recovering your heart. Allow yourself to trust other people are making their own conscious decisions to receive from the abundance of the universe. Allow yourself to realize you are in the presence of your being and becoming.

∽ *Tezet 144*

Being is not something you have to ask for as a human being. Allow yourself to become conscious of giving your attention to your steps and movements. Allow yourself to become conscious of moving in humility. Remember to walk in grace and kindness. Allow yourself to see the elegance of your being as a creation of the Creator. Allow yourself to become conscious of how it feels to be in alignment with Creation.

∽ *Tezet 145*

As you become conscious of yourself moving and functioning in alignment with Creation, allow yourself to acknowledge the clarity you have in your ability to live in a state of transformation—being and becoming. Allow yourself to become conscious of the gentleness you share with other people. Show the process of your being and becoming through the ways you are being in your most intimate relationships. Through the reflection you offer, allow yourself to be present as a guidepost for other people as they walk toward the path of self-acceptance. Become conscious of the ways you touch the lives of people close to you. Allow yourself to not be self-absorbed by seeing the fullness of humanity near and far.

∽ *Tezet 146*

Allow yourself to realize how your actions impact all of those who are connected to you. Allow yourself to become conscious and know you have the ability to be a gift to all that you come into contact with. Allow yourself to see how your process of being and becoming gives you the capacity to share peace with other people. Allow yourself to realize your love is a gift you are offering toward the advancement of humanity. Allow yourself to see yourself as light. As you come into the fullness of being light, remember lightness is not a burden, but a gift meant to lift humanity. Allow yourself to experience heaviness as a guide to teach you how to release the fear of transforming, being, and becoming. In becoming conscious of yourself you are learning and realizing all people share in the lightness and heaviness of being a conduit of the Creator and Creation.

∽ *Tezet 147*

Remember peace is gained through the exploration of what has produced the pain in your life. Allow yourself to know, as you have been given knowledge, you are expected to develop the knowledge of yourself. Allow yourself to see what has given you the ability to be strong and resilient. As you grow into yourself other people will begin to the see authenticity of the love and peace you are sharing. Allow yourself to see you are a channel of transformation, being, and becoming. Allow yourself to see the challenges you face in your life and living are not insurmountable.

◆ *Tezet 148*

Allow yourself to seek comfort in being with the people closest to you. Your relationships and connections allow you to see the blessing you are to other people. Allow yourself to know the process of transformation, being, and becoming are eternal processes that will always be with you. Allow yourself to become conscious of how Creation is providing for you. Allow yourself to realize the process of being is the process of perfecting who you have been called to be in this lifetime. Allow yourself to create space and time to share the peace and pain of your life and living.

◆ *Tezet 149*

Do not allow the ego to mock the personality emerging from within your heart. Allow yourself to be joyful as you begin to relate to the inner being that is emerging. Allow yourself to consider who you are becoming, as you accept your path of development. Allow yourself to consider the goodness you are realizing, as you learn to connect with the source. Allow yourself to realize you are surrounded by good people who care about your life and living. Remember justice (maat) as an ancient principle is here to guide you toward the Self.

∽ *Tezet 150*

Remember, all the places and spaces you have encountered freedom, help you discover a part of you. Because you are light, allow yourself to radiate with the love of the divine presence. Allow yourself to walk in the goodness of being a reflection of justice and light in the world. Allow yourself to realize you are called to become conscious of yourself as a channel for the Creator to be present on earth and in the heavens. As you realize the inner source of your being, allow the image of the divine to be present in the daily actions of your life and living. Allow love to become the voice of truth that speaks from within your being.

∽ *Tezet 151*

Maat is the principle of truth, balance, justice, reciprocity, rightness, order, and harmony.

Being
Transformation

Being and Becoming Tezet:
Affirmations and Allowances

As you become conscious of yourself, become consciously aware of the people you come across in the process of your development. Allow yourself to walk through life working toward being a good person to the people you meet. Remember, good people are conscious of themselves, and other people, as beings connected to the source of Creation. Allow yourself to consider what it means to see yourself a human being. Remember, you are learning to offer love as a statement of who you are becoming as a conscious being. Allow yourself to remember the goodness that has been shared with you as you have worked towards living with a light heart.

◆ *Tezet 152*

As you increase the consciousness of who you are being and who you are becoming, allow yourself to feel pride in being a person who considers the wellbeing of other human beings. Being conscious of your own sense of sharing goodness with the world, allows you to demonstrate the power of being human. Allow yourself to realize at your core, there is a reflection of the excellence visible in Creation. In your becoming conscious of the qualities that make people function, you will increase your inner sight and wisdom. Allow yourself to live well as you learn to live within the makings of who you are called to be. In becoming conscious of the Creator within you, allow yourself to rise above the ways you have lived in opposition to yourself before now and realize there is nothing to be forgiven.

◆ *Tezet 153*

Allow yourself to live in the qualities that allow you to feel a greater sense of being human. Allow your heart to be light with the fullness of grace given to you, as you recover your consciousness of the divine presence in Creation. Allow yourself to see there is no need to forgive yourself for learning to walk on the path that has been placed before you to teach you who you are. Allow yourself to realize knowledge of yourself is at the basis of your life and living. As you realize the knowledge of who you are, allow yourself to see how all people are created through the divine presence in Creation. In realizing you are a reflection of the divine presence in Creation, you will realize people are not created to live in isolation and disconnection.

❧ *Tezet 154*

Allow yourself to know you are light. Connect with other people with the aim of encountering and sharing peace. In learning to connect with other people, you will discover there are times when the journey into humanity can feel heavy. Part of the lesson you are learning is anchored in knowing your peace cannot be filled with burdens. Allow yourself to discover the richness in understanding and resolving sadness, grief, and mourning. In learning to share a life of love with other people, you will become conscious of allowing yourself to release the heaviness of being forced to live in isolation.

❧ *Tezet 155*

As you discover the power of your will, consider how you respond to the people closest to you. Allow yourself to see the depth of the impact you are having on the relationships you are attempting to grow in your becoming. Allow yourself to become conscious of your needs and the needs of the people closest to you as you create space for there to be an increase in harmony between you. Allow yourself to become conscious of the need for harmony as you learn to share in the calling to build community together. Allow yourself to feel the need to be alone in your process of becoming conscious of your transformation. Allow yourself to begin to approach your life and living with space to discover what is required to be in lasting relationship with other people.

❧ *Tezet 156*

Allow yourself to become conscious of the choices you are making to create space for understanding and closeness. Allow yourself to see you are connected to other people through your ability to be grounded in the knowledge of your heart. Through the practice of sharing your thoughts and experiences, allow yourself to discover what your bonds are made of. Allow your heart to teach you how to consider your connection to other people. Allow yourself to create spaces to contemplate the level of attention you give your connections. In your becoming conscious of being, allow yourself to be open to evolution and the development of your feelings and thoughts.

❧ *Tezet 157*

Allow yourself to see the interconnectedness of hope and knowledge. Allow yourself to begin to love what you are discovering as you learn what relationships are made of. In your being and becoming, allow yourself to realize the intentionality required to give life to the relationships you will develop as a part of the emergence of yourself. Allow yourself to begin to be at ease as you consider new ways of seeing how relationships function. Allow yourself to become conscious of the attention you are giving to creating vision for your relationships. Allow yourself to see the importance of giving yourself permission to work toward allowing other people to support you, as you are discovering what it means to not live an isolated existence.

≼ *Tezet 158*

As you grow into the fullness of your being, remember all the people who have invested in your being and becoming. Give yourself permission to work through the pain you have experienced as a result of the fragmentation you witnessed during the process of your becoming. Allow yourself to see the impact of not tending to the relationship with your heart. Allow yourself to see the ability to develop strength in your connections with other people when you give yourself permission to be present with the conditions of your heart. In your being and becoming, you will discover your relationships mirror your internal life and living. As you discover the power of being connected to the function of your heart, allow yourself to seek balance in being in relationship with other people.

≼ *Tezet 159*

Allow yourself to realize knowledge of the Self is at the core of what you are being and becoming. Allow yourself to consider the associations you make in the process of discovering who you are and who your people are. It is in realizing you are made into a human in relationship with other human beings, that gives you permission to accept the presence you are being called to share with other people. Allow yourself to become conscious of the healing you are seeking, as you work to have a life and living anchored in freedom. Allow yourself to visualize yourself as a symbol of peace, balance, and harmony.

∼ *Tezet 160*

In your life and living, you give meaning to the human ability to rise above the aspects of regret and shame created to disconnect you from the source of your being. As you live, you are allowing yourself to give birth to the strength the Ancestors have left for us in their transformations into spirit. As you come into the conscious awareness of yourself, see the freedom placed inside your heart as a beacon for your life's work of being and becoming. Allow yourself to work on deepening your relationships with the Ancestors, as you learn to channel the teachings from their experience of having been present on the planet. Allow yourself to become conscious of giving your attention to the knowledge that holds you in union with the Ancestors. Allow yourself to become an expression of the eternal connection we all share with the divine and all that is divine in Creation.

∼ *Tezet 161*

In your becoming you are learning to learn from your process of being. In your becoming you are learning to learn from the gift being born in this form, as a human being. In becoming aware of yourself as a spiritual presence allow yourself to realize there is cosmic truth and eternal peace in being. Allow yourself to find comfort in knowing you are connected to the Creator and to all of the great Ancestors who have called you into being. Allow yourself to feel the gift of being that exists beyond the physical space of living and allow yourself to move towards the eternal wisdom working to live through you. In your becoming conscious of the knowledge you have about life and living allow yourself to give birth to the growth and expansion found in the cycles of being, becoming, and transformation.

ᴥ *Tezet 162*

In the evolution of your consciousness allow yourself to release the fear attached to facing the unknown—to unleash the power of human existence. Allow yourself to discover the sense of power that was birthed in your decision to be born into your current state of being. Allow yourself to realize you are not afraid as you discover the comfort in knowing the truth of your purpose and calling. As you become conscious of yourself as a human being, allow this process to support the awareness of being that is emerging from being consciously aware of what you are being called to become. Do not allow yourself to believe you can be disconnected from the source of being as you work to unravel the sound of your heartbeat from the noise of the world. It is in your being and becoming conscious of yourself you are given deeper understanding of the universe.

∾ *Tezet 163*

In the spaces you have created for yourself, become intentional in placing reminders that reinforce your realization you are a reflection of the divine in Creation. Allow yourself to realize you are the love of Creation. Allow yourself to become conscious of Creation's desire to demonstrate love toward the collective human family through the reflection of your being and becoming. Know yourself and know you are an expression of the Creator. Allow yourself to leave space for discovering the fullness of becoming aware of the newness created through your being present on the planet. Allow yourself to study the transformations as reminders of the processes that have taken place, as a result of your ability to face all of the stages of your being and becoming.

∾ *Tezet 164*

Allow yourself to imagine journeying through life with a light heart. As you learn to live in sync with Creation, give yourself permission to release the sense of being overwhelmed by the unexpected aspects of living. Allow yourself to become conscious of the storms you have endured before now. Allow yourself to create space to pause in the wonder of being an enduring soul. As you learn to follow your heart, do not forget you are in pursuit of your destiny. As you become conscious of yourself as an enduring soul, open your mind to seeing how your life's mission is a cosmic reflection.

⋖ *Tezet 165*

As you learn to live in community with other people, take note of what gives you comfort in your life and living. Allow yourself to imagine how you might grow a deeper sense of comfort with how your heart is calling you to live in union with other people. Allow the growth you experience in your life and living to become an opening to experience the gift of having peace in relationship to all of humanity. In your becoming conscious of your capacity for being, you will begin to discover life is full of unimaginable possibilities. In your becoming conscious of your life's mission, you will discover you were designed to endure what life and living offers to you. Allow yourself to push beyond the limits you have placed on yourself before now and become the person you are being called to be.

⋖ *Tezet 166*

In the process of your becoming aware of the oneness of your own timelessness, allow yourself to become amazed with every step you take towards knowing the unknown. Allow yourself to become aware of the light that is emanating from your being, and know you and the lightness of being are one. Allow yourself to be embraced by the light in order to see the light and dark are one. Allow your heart to guide you beyond the false idea you cannot face the unknown, into the knowledge of being one with the Spirit of Creation. Allow yourself to consider the potential you symbolize for all of humanity. Allow yourself to give birth to the newness present in the light of your own divine spark.

∽ *Tezet 167*

In your becoming, do not allow conformity to restrict who and what you are being or becoming. Allow yourself to move beyond allowing the process of being to be perceived as being difficult and allow yourself to discover the presence of ease in your being. Allow yourself to realize the decision to become present in your being is not incidental or random. In the journey inward you will discover the truth held in your potential as you choose to live a life of oneness within yourself and with the outside world. Allow yourself to see the wisdom in considering the path of your own enlightenment. In living a life of consciousness, allow yourself to be present in the being that is being called forward from within your heart; allow your being to be what it is.

∽ *Tezet 168*

There is a beauty in the realization your being is a choice made before this present moment. Allow yourself to seek the fullness of your potential through the studying of yourself in relationship to what is above and below. Do not allow yourself to create challenges for yourself by questioning what you are being called to be. Allow yourself to see all the potential that surrounds you and allow yourself to be the manifestation of the Creator's greatest potential for humanity. Allow yourself to see and embrace the gift in being. Hold the presence of your being in reverence, as you discover the oneness of your being in relationship to the divine presence that has called you into being.

∽ *Tezet 169*

Allow yourself to become conscious of moving into your being. As you move toward the consciousness of being, realize truth for humanity is anchored in universal forces. Allow yourself to see your humanity is made present in every choice you make toward building a presence of harmony and unity. Allow yourself to become conscious of your ability to see the reality you and your people are facing. It is in your ability to see your ways of being that will create the conditions for harmony on the planet. Allow yourself to become conscious of how all aspects of your life teach you to see freedom.

∽ *Tezet 170*

It is in realizing there are no coincidences you will develop the sight to realize all you are being bombarded with from outside of yourself. It is in learning to live with a light heart you allow yourself to realize peace as the source of your capacity to experience life and living in alignment with the harmony present in Creation. Allow yourself to take moments to realize what has produced the consciousness you are experiencing. Allow yourself to accept the consciousness of what is being asked of your as you consider your being and becoming. In realizing your ability to be you, you will see how Creation and the Creator have given you a life filled with freedom. Allow yourself to realize the freedom of the Creator and Creation are in conscious pursuit of your consciousness.

∽ *Tezet 171*

Allow yourself to realize it is when you allow the Self to be present you are truly being. Allow yourself to see how you are being given choices to teach you to see your internal reality as the source of your ability live in peace. Be present in listening to your heart and allow your mind to be clear of uncertainty. Allow yourself to know you do not lack sight or insight. In allowing yourself to see yourself with knowledge, you will realize you are responsible for what you make of your life and living. Allow your life to be filled with insight.

∽ *Tezet 172*

Allow yourself to be open to realizing being comes to you as potential. By living in your potential, you will see the gift in choosing to take the journey of developing yourself. In learning to be present, you will realize what it means to have self-knowledge. Allow yourself to be free to see all the possibilities in self-development. Open your heart and mind to embracing the visions that surface as you allow the next steps toward your becoming to be revealed. In accepting the knowledge and development of yourself, you will realize you can have a life and living grounded in self-love.

∽ *Tezet 173*

Allow yourself to be open to your inner wisdom. Allow your insight to show you who you are. In realizing the fullness of who you are, see yourself and rejoice. Be present with your heart and know you are being called to release your potential. Do not hold yourself back from becoming, realize and unleash your power to transform your existence. Show those closest to you what you are realizing about the presence of your being.

❧ *Tezet 174*

Allow yourself to see and realize the choices the Creator has made available to you. Allow yourself to begin your journey toward being with the knowledge of being. Open your heart and mind to seeing what your journey is offering you. Allow yourself the freedom to dream without limits or boundaries. As you realize your dreams, open yourself up to living beyond a path of suffering. Allow yourself to remember the freedoms you felt as a child and be present in the consciousness of your youth.

❧ *Tezet 175*

Allow yourself to become conscious of your will. Allow yourself to be present in the presence of being who you are willing to be. In becoming conscious of yourself, you will discover nothing outside of freedom is an acceptable way to live. Allow yourself to realize the images your being has held for you to become. Release the tension of living with drudgery as you discover the gift in the rituals and ceremonies that ground you. Release the Self and allow love to be present for your growth.

❧ *Tezet 176*

It is the Neter Tehuti, who keeps record of the movement of the Creative Consciousness through its becoming.

It is this consciousness in the process of its becoming that ultimately produces man.

It is the active consciousness of Creator in Creation that leads man (kem).

Consciousness is the temple in man.

Becoming the Source

Being and Becoming Tezet:
Affirmations and Allowances

Allow yourself to take time to be in the process of studying your inner knowledge. Allow yourself to relate to and heal your inner child. In healing your inner child, you are working to create hope from some of your earliest experiences with life and living. Allow yourself to see your relentless nature to live with a passion toward freedom. In healing your inner child, you will discover you have always been free. Allow your inner child to reteach you how to choose to live in the freedom created in you by the Creator. Allow yourself to see your being through the healing of the child within.

❧ *Tezet 177*

Allow yourself to see how you are the journey. As you move towards your higher states of consciousness, embrace your inner child. Allow yourself to hold your inner child in the most sacred space in your heart. Allow yourself to remember the things that comforted you and gave you the strength to endure to your present state. Remember the pain you are experiencing is a part of the growth of becoming. As you release yourself from the pain, free your inner child.

❧ *Tezet 178*

As you become conscious of what you have lived through, remember your inner child has never left you. Allow yourself to care for your inner child as you learn to accept yourself as a human being. As you release the teaching of your inner child, offer your freedom as a way for other people to discover theirs, while also seeing yours as a symbol of your relentlessness. Allow yourself to see how you are free to live without fear. Your inner child has used all the gifts you have been given from Creation to endure. See how you have not been left alone and embrace the images of the child within. Allow yourself to realize the dreams of your inner child have been given to you as a part of your path toward freedom.

◈ *Tezet 179*

Allow yourself to dream of the times when you allowed yourself to experience real freedom. Allow yourself to be in the presence of your most sacred self and remember the freedom you have experienced beyond the limitations you have faced. Allow yourself to recall your first breath of being conscious and remember your day of birth. Allow yourself to see how committed you have been to your being and becoming. Allow yourself to understand what teachings you were being given at your beginning. Allow yourself to remember the importance of imagination and knowledge.

◈ *Tezet 180*

Allow yourself to become conscious of the spirit that is present inside of your presence. Allow yourself to be present in the light of the day. Give yourself permission to recreate the ways of your being, as you learn to travel the path you have been given. Allow yourself to see each day as a place to begin. Allow yourself to bring forth the peace and the wisdom of your inner child. Allow yourself to see the importance of your inner child, as you learn to see the strength of generations inside of your being.

◈ *Tezet 181*

Allow yourself to realize your inner child was present before you were called into being. Remember how you began. Remember the journey you have been on. Allow yourself to see the journey you have taken and the knowledge you have produced on life's journey. Allow yourself to see how, through your learning, you will be given the ability to realize your dreams. Allow your heart to be open to considering your dreams and allow your dreams to give you insight into how you are being.

✍ *Tezet 182*

Allow yourself to see how you have developed the strength that allows you to see you are strong. Remember to see the light of your being is clear. Allow yourself to see how your inner child is waiting to be freed through the presence of your being. Allow yourself to discover your inner child as you rediscover yourself. Allow yourself to be the Self the Creator created in the beginning.

✍ *Tezet 183*

Allow yourself to learn and know all that life has to offer you. Allow yourself to know freedom is experienced in the ways you choose to follow your dreams. As you learn to follow your heart, allow yourself to realize worry and anxiety have their place in learning to trust the Self. You are not different from the rest of Creation, being is a part of your design. In learning how you are being, allow yourself to understand your inner child. Allow yourself to create space to sit in the presence of your inner child.

✍ *Tezet 184*

Allow yourself to have a life free of the limits of worry and fear. See how worry and fear are used to keep you from your dreams. Allow yourself to be aware of danger in the world, but do not allow worry and fear to prevent you from living. Allow yourself to live from a place of awareness and consciousness. Do not allow fear to prevent you from taking the journey into the unknown parts of realizing your dreams. Allow yourself to use awareness and knowledge to guide you toward freedom. Allow yourself to find freedom in the peace you have been given. Allow yourself to realize there is no fear in your peace.

∞ *Tezet 185*

Allow yourself to see how obsessing over worry is a distraction from being. In becoming conscious of how you are living and being know you have the ability to develop trust in your being and becoming. In allowing yourself to become aware of yourself as a being and you grow into what you have been called to become. Allow your being to transform pain and suffering. Allow yourself to trust the process of what you are becoming. Allow yourself to release worry and begin to live.

∞ *Tezet 186*

In becoming aware of yourself, know you have the capacity to return to the things that have distracted you in the past; you also have the ability to stay focused and advance your life and living. Allow yourself to unleash and release the freedom you discover in connecting with your inner child. Allow your heart and mind to always come back to the peace Creation created you out of. Allow yourself to remember the Creator is being channeled through your life and living. Allow yourself to become conscious of how sharing concern and empathy for yourself supports the growth of compassion you have for other people. Become ever mindful of how peace is released through you as a part of your capacity to presence the divine in your being and becoming.

∞ *Tezet 187*

Allow yourself to release the voice holding you back and lean into the voice calling you to move toward freedom. In your freedom, realize your peace is a realization the Creator has given you as a way of allowing you to become conscious of the value in being you. Allow yourself to come to a place where your greatest concern is the way you are being with yourself in your being. Allow the peace of the Creator to be realized through your presence and being. Allow yourself to become conscious of the realization that your spirit is pure—you are pure. Allow yourself to realize you are the purest form of freedom Creation has given to the planet. Allow yourself to become conscious of your connection to time and begin to shape the reality of the spaces your will moves through.

∞ *Tezet 188*

Allow yourself to become conscious of your ability to rise above the momentary distractions created from the process of life and living. Remember it is the peace of the Creator and Creation you are being called to create through your presence. Allow yourself to realize you are in the process of learning how being and becoming are made present through peace. In learning to have a presence of peace, you are learning to express the peace of being human. Allow yourself to be an expression of love as a reflection of the Creator's empathy. Allow yourself to embrace the peace in remembering to share concern for other people.

❧ *Tezet 189*

Allow yourself to remember the freedom held in your process of being and becoming. Allow yourself to experience understanding in your being and becoming. Allow yourself to know you will come in contact with people who thinking differently about what it means to be human beings. Allow yourself to accept the truth of realizing you are on the perfecting journey created to reflect the process of the Creator's being and becoming. Allow yourself space to express freedom. Allow yourself space to know you are an image in the mirror of Creation.

❧ *Tezet 190*

Allow yourself to become what is left after worry has left you. Allow yourself to realize you are only as worried and anxious as you allow yourself to be or become. Allow yourself to settle into the peace you are being and becoming. Allow your spirit to live freely through your being and becoming. Allow yourself to realize the beauty and wonder you are presencing through your being and becoming.

❧ *Tezet 191*

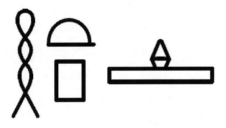

Hotep is the word for peace. It is a cake upon a mat or offering table.

Concluding with Gratitude

Being and Becoming Tezet:
Affirmations and Allowances

I choose to conclude this text with gratitude for the guidance and support of Elder Atum Azzahir, Founder and Executive Director of the Cultural Wellness Center. I first met Elder Atum in 2006. When I first heard her, I was in awe. I was in awe of her ability to speak the truth. I was not aware of what was behind her words, or that there was even a teaching that she subscribed to. It was her presence. In her presence I felt like a whole person. I felt seen and heard by someone outside of my mother. This was not a feeling I was accustomed to allowing myself to feel.

Meeting Elder Atum was life-transforming because of the wisdom she shared with me in those early years of our relationship. My first meeting with her one-on-one was at the Cultural Wellness Center when it was located on Bloomington and Lake Street. In our first meetings I remember being received with the love and openness of a mother. My life was in crisis at that time. I was in a spiritually lonely and low place. I remember sitting with her and feeling open to share with her the place I found myself in. I wanted to share with her how lost I felt. I had not yet learned the words to describe my experience. There was no way to know what I did not know. And even though I didn't say what was fully on my heart, I still felt heard by her.

We talked about my life as a professional and what I wanted for myself. She shared with me the People's Theory and stated, "Individualism, loss of culture, and loss of community are what make you sick," and the mission of the Cultural Wellness Center is to, "unleash the power of people to heal themselves and build community." I was enthralled by the way she thought and the kind of freedom she exuded. Here was this beautiful and strong feminine presence, expressing to me a way out of the pain and the suffering. I began to see her as a wise sage who had the words for the experience I was having and her solution was to turn the pain and suffering into knowledge.

The experience stuck with me. She had this small office and I remember being so interested in the piles of books and stacks of papers that surrounded us—it was like she knew where everything was. She would have a thought and she would reach toward a stack and come out with a response to a question I had posed or a thought we were sharing. I left her office one day only to lose contact with her for about a year. When we connected again, I felt myself be a bit more open about where I was in my life. I had spiraled further into a professional crisis and was ready let go of where I was living to learn how to live in balance with myself - to live in peace with myself and the people closest to me.

I found myself sitting with her many times over the years simply to ask her about how to know myself better—I think this may be the reason she offered me to join her in a class at the International Khepran Institute in the fall of 2007. Maybe she knew I was in search of my own divine presence. Maybe she knew I was in search of *tezet*. Maybe she knew I was in search of transformation—being and becoming. I have a deep realization she is aware, and was aware that all of us—Black people in the Americas—are in search of transformation. I know she knew I was in search of Khepra.

In meeting Elder Atum, I was introduced to Seba Ahmad, the teachings of *tezet* - seeing the Self as a reflection of the Divine

Presence in Creation and to see myself as a person who is conscious of the eternal consciousness inside of myself. It was Elder Atum's guidance and the teachings of the Cultural Wellness Center I would come to depend on as I explored what it means to live in harmony with my personal khepra. Her presence was teaching me to see the potential in seeing myself as a reflection of the divine presence in Creation. Her instructions were simple and clear—you have to learn to slow down, you have to learn to study yourself, and you have to learn how to tell yourself the truth. Each person must know who they are and what their purpose and function is on the planet and this process does not happen in isolation. During my time at the Cultural Wellness Center, I have learned to see the practices of my life as the tools to get me through the anguish present in the mundane.

In a very important way, I have learned we are all in search of seeing a world that is not driven by suffering and pain. We are all in search of life and living that exists outside of the brutality of living in the world we experience daily. I was in search of something inside of me that was eternal, truthful, and real. I was looking for a sustainable life and a way to live in the splendor and beauty of being alive. I realize this morning, as I am writing these words, I felt dead inside. All of the things I did to cover the pain and to mask the suffering only made it worse. I was consumed by life in the modern world, and it felt as though it was consuming my soul with every step I took.

What I have found and am finding is, as we learn to live in better ways we learn to live in greater peace and harmony with ourselves and the people closest to us. I am using the expression

the people closest to us intentionally. This is intentional because as
we learn to have peaceful relationships with the people closest
to our hearts, we learn to be in relationship with the world in
the same way. I feel a sense of naivete in myself as these words
hit the page, but I believe hope is a need. It is a part of the
process of learning to trust yourself and to trust the voice that
is coming through you. I want to express beauty. I want to see
beautiful things being expressed in the world. In a way, this is
part of the journey I am on. The words shared here are my
attempt to feel a sense of solidity within myself.

I will forever be grateful to Elder Atum and the divine work
of creating space for people of African heritage to heal through
the work of the Cultural Wellness Center. It has been her eldering
and guidance that has allowed me to create space and time to
consider what it means for me to heal myself and to build community. It has been her presence that has silently urged me to a
place of being willing and able to share my voice with the people
closest to me. The point of this self-study in the beginning was
for me to learn to affirm my own presence in the world. It was
her knowledge and wisdom that was quietly affirming me. Elder
Atum cared for me with her instructions and teachings about the
struggle and experiences of Black people. As I listened, I began
to learn to love and accept myself as a human being. I learned to
accept myself as a reflection of the divine in Creation.

Each sentence in this self-study comes from the intelligence
of my heart. The intelligence comes from my willingness to
consider the divine that exists in the world and my willingness
to see those closest to me as the reflection of the divine in Cre-

ation. This teaches me to be true to the wisdom I hold within my heart. The wisdom of my heart taught me to protect my heart and to keep it open at the same time. I never ever really wanted to share my thoughts and feelings publicly because sharing my feelings in general make me feel vulnerable. However, I have learned to accept the role vulnerability can play in the healing process. It has been within the context of my personal healing process I have learned one very important teaching I have taken from Elder Atum, and I share with you—*you have to get up each day and do what the forces in Creation are asking of you because it is the process of your life that creates the product.*

Finally, I would like to end by expressing gratitude and thanks to you as you have spent time with the reflections from my heart. I pray you appreciate the voice you discover as you begin to commit yourself to your own practice of *creating a space for presence.* I pray the daily practice of writing six sentences provides you with a disciplined practice toward realizing the peace and ease possible in both mind and spirit. I pray in the days, weeks, months, or years you will spend with this self-study text, you learn to value what you discover inside yourself.

I pray these affirmations and allowances allow you to make space to realize you are the light in the dark you are in search of. I pray you allow yourself to become aware of yourself as a reflection of the divine in Creation. I pray these expressions have a peaceful, motivating impact on the person you are writing to accept, and I pray you realize the person you are being called to become.

Allow yourself to write every day.

Works Cited

Being and Becoming Tezet:
Affirmations and Allowances

Azzahir, A. (2001). *Time Dimensions and Community Development.* International Khepran Institute.

Azzahir, A., Azzahir, A., & Nefer-Ra, N. (2003). *The Student of Khepra Manual.* International Khepran Institute.

Azzahir, A. (2006). *International Khepran Institute Course Bulletin.* International Khepran Institute.

Azzahir, A. (2017). *The Three Books of Khepra: A Khepran Knowledge Philosophy.* International Khephran Institute.

Azzahir, A. (2019). *Reseach and the Cultural Wellness Center.* International Khepran Institute.

Azzahir, A., Azzahir, A., & Tezet, M. (2019). *Seeds of Greatness Within Blackness.* Cultural Wellness Center.

Wilson, A., (2019). *The Psychology of Self-hatred and Self-defeat: Towards a Reclamation of the Afrikan Mind.* Afrikan World InfoSystems.